TO FULFILL THIS MINISTRY

TO FULFILL
THIS MINISTRY

❧

WILLIAM C. MARTIN

Abingdon Press
New York • *Nashville*

TO FULFILL THIS MINISTRY

Copyright MCMXLIX by Pierce & Smith

Library of Congress Catalog Card Number: 49-7610

G

SET UP, PRINTED, AND BOUND BY THE
PARTHENON PRESS, AT NASHVILLE,
TENNESSEE, UNITED STATES OF AMERICA

TO SALLIE

PREFACE

THIS IS A PLAIN BOOK ABOUT PRACTICAL MATTERS. IT IS THE outflowing of the conviction that the measure of the Church's strength in any generation is the fidelity and effectiveness of its pastoral ministry. The only justification for venturing into a field that has been so repeatedly and so thoroughly explored is the need to bring into vital relationship certain elements of parish responsibility which are under special demand today.

This is not a comprehensive survey of the life and activity of the local congregation. However, the pastoral obligations which are dealt with are so basic that when they are properly discharged every other duty will be simplified and made easier. There is no need to insist upon agreement in nonessentials. But the pastor is not prepared to fulfill his ministry with skill and confidence until he has arrived at conclusions of his own about the areas of responsibility brought under review here.

These chapters took form at the time when the world was shaken by the violence of global conflict and were completed in the midst of the tensions which dominate it today. The absence of frequent reference to these events is not a result of failure to appreciate their implications for the Church during the days ahead. It is rather an indirect declaration of faith that there are deathless elements in the Church and its ministry which, with variations incited by centuries and cultures, will endure to the end of the ages.

There is no way to present ideas like these without being autobiographical. This is dangerous procedure, I know, in a day when so many young pastors are familiar with the methods of psychoanalysis, but I am taking the risk.

The book would never have been written if I had not agreed, with characteristic ministerial alacrity, to deliver the Willson lectures at McMurry College. My thanks to Mr. and Mrs. J. M. Willson for establishing the lectureship; to President Harold G. Cooke and the committee for the invitation to speak; to the faculty, students, and visiting ministers for providing an appreciative audience; and to the pastors of Kansas and Nebraska with whom I have worked, and in whose lives and ministry I have witnessed a devotion which has made it easy for me to write hopefully about our calling.

WILLIAM C. MARTIN

CONTENTS

I

WE HAVE THIS MINISTRY

THE PASTORAL OVERSIGHT OF A LOCAL PARISH STANDS AT the heart of the Christian ministry. Everything that is written in this book grows directly out of this basic conviction. It is important to keep in mind that the terms "pastor" and "pastoral" are here used in the wider sense of including all the duties that relate to the administration of a parish.

The correctness of this appraisal of the pastoral ministry might be challenged by a reminder that it is not in accord with the order of priority given in the New Testament. You will recall that there the succession goes like this: first, apostles; then, prophets; then, evangelists and, finally, pastors and teachers. The reply to such an objection is that in a completely adequate conception of the pastoral ministry all these forms of Christian outreach are bound up together. When the pastor of today undertakes a piece of courageous pioneering—within his parish or beyond it— he is engaged in apostolic business. When he gives fearless interpretation to the Christian gospel in terms of present-day living, he is discharging the obligation of a prophet. When he presents Christ to the people in such a way that they feel impelled to commit their lives to him as Redeemer and Lord, he is doing the work of an evangelist.

Here the Church wins or loses

It is within the borders of the local parish that the Church makes immediate contact with its field of operation. If it succeeds here, its work is effective; if it fails, the failure is complete. Every denominational agency, institutional or personal, is maintained in order that the labors of the pastor, here or in another land, may be more productive.

Kenneth S. Latourette says: "The office of the Christian pastor is unique. It is a distinctively and peculiarly Christian creation. In China, for example, the office of teacher has long been known and held in high esteem. Anything corresponding to the Christian pastor, however, with his love of human souls and his sacrificial shepherding of individuals in weal and in woe, is unknown. A leading American pastor has described the office as being that of 'the inspired, trained, and accredited friend at large of the community.' A profession embodying just this combination of ideals is alien to every faith except Christianity. Its creation is essential if we are to see successful, continuing Christian communities." [1]

There is no completely dependable method of computing the force of the Church's impact upon our American life in this generation. One of the most accurate answers to the question would be found if it could be determined to what extent the 140,000 pastors in this country—Jewish, Catholic, and Protestant—are committed with wholehearted devotion to their calling. To what degree are they recognizing in the pastoral ministry the opportunity of

[1] *Missions Tomorrow* (New York, Harper & Bros., 1936), p. 176.

using to the fullest measure their gifts and training? To what extent are they finding that the requirements of parish duties are contributing to their inner demand for continuing growth and development? What is the measure of enthusiastic release with which they are pouring their best resources into the daily round of their ministrations?

Not infrequently, a pastor lets it be known that he is interested in a more executive position. After due allowance is made for the importance of the place into which he wishes to go, there is often good reason to suspect that the deeper basis of his desire for a change is that he has grown tired of the drudgery and the limitations of pastoral work. His patience has worn thin by dealing with slow-footed and recalcitrant church officials. The obligation to prepare two new sermons every week has grown monotonous. The business of visiting sick people and pacifying disgruntled church members has become a weariness of the flesh. And the constant demand for statistical reports and all the other endless round of details is an irritating hindrance to the growth of the soul which can hardly be tolerated. If only he could find a place in the Church where he could be master of his own schedule and where he would not be so constantly subjected to the whims of inconsiderate people— a place where a man could have wider contacts and where the deadening routine of small duties did not stifle him— then the talents that have been entrusted to him could really be developed and he could do something of permanent worth for the Kingdom. Recently I read of a pastor who had been offered a teaching position in a church college. He was debating whether he should accept the invitation. And then the answer crystallized in favor of the college after an evening with his official board in which the members hesitated about adopting the proposal for an addition to the church building. The way of escape was at hand.

The value of specialized work in the Church should not be discounted. Much of it simply must be done, in a complex age like ours, if the Church is to fulfill its mission. But the ground upon which the real battle is ultimately lost or won is not an executive office, remote from the hearts and homes of the people, but the area of a parish, small or large, where individuals and groups are enmeshed in the fierce tensions of good and evil and where vital choices are made. When a Christian minister, no matter what the nature of his special appointment may be, loses the heart of a pastor he is largely disqualified for any assignment by the Church which relates to the welfare of people.

"Except they be sent"

There are three conditions essential to an effective and joyous pastoral ministry. The first is a *valid and continuing call* to be a minister of Christ. It is sufficient to say with regard to the nature of the call to the ministry that God honors our individuality in revealing his will as it relates to our vocation. I am sure that I have heard or read the experiences of at least fifty men with respect to this call and no two of them were alike. The important thing about the call to preach is not the form but the reality of it. To some it comes with the dramatic suddenness of a flash of lightning in a dark night. To others it comes like the quiet dawning of the day. The calmer experience is as real and as valid as the more spectacular one and, in spite of certain contrary notions, it has always been the predominant type. The point of emphasis here is that no man is prepared to face the demands of the Christian ministry with courage and confidence until he is certain, in his own heart, that God has chosen and sent him.

The Protestant Church through various recruiting agencies is at last making an intelligent effort to acquaint carefully selected young men with the opportunities of service offered by the Christian ministry. This is a movement worthy of generous encouragement. If, however, the results of this search for recruits are to be worthy of the Christian tradition, certain safeguards are essential. It must be understood by those who speak and by those who hear that the purpose of such conferences is limited to the consideration of the opportunities and demands of the ministry. The impression must be strictly avoided that the wisest discernment of men can ever be substituted for the voice of God. There is danger that an acute shortage of ministers, such as we face today, may betray us into the use of superficial methods for securing recruits which would be hurtful both to individuals and to the Church, and would lead to bitter regrets tomorrow.

A ministry that is self-appointed on the basis of the recognition of need on the one hand and of special gifts on the other might do well enough, from the human point of view, if there could be an assurance of fair weather for the entire voyage. But the course of this ministry does not run through such a sea. When the storm breaks, a man needs for a compass something more than an awareness of the evil of the world and a benevolent desire to be helpful. He needs to know that it was God who set him on this journey and that he dare not turn back. This conviction can sustain a man in his high calling when everything else fails him. An anchor that will hold is an experience to which he can turn in his hour of testing and say, "Here God touched my life. Since he did that for me, how can I doubt that he will do yet more?"

When Amos went up from the ranch country of Tekoa to tell the city dwellers of Bethel the kind of righteousness that God demanded, he was not well received. The power that enabled him to stand against the scorn and indifference of the people and the fierce denunciation of Amaziah, the priest, was the fact that he could say, "God took me from following the flock and sent me here to speak this word." The force that held John Frederick Oberlin in a country parish of the Vosges Mountains for nearly sixty years was the conviction that God had a special work for him to do in that place. The assurance that he was where God wanted him to be enabled him to say, "I do not want to labor in some quiet pastoral charge where I can be at ease. I want a work which no one else wishes to do and which will not be done unless I do it." When John Bunyan had been in jail for nearly twelve years for preaching the truth as God revealed it to him, the jailer came one day and said, "John, you can go free if you'll agree to quit preaching." Bunyan's reply is a treasured heritage of the Protestant faith: "I am determined, Almighty God being my help and shield, yet to suffer, if frail life might continue so long, even till the moss shall grow over my eyebrows, rather than to violate my faith and make a continual butchery of my conscience." The prophetic element of the pastoral ministry can be discharged only by men whose commission transcends the will of man.

Someone may insist that this standard of the ministry is so high that it will be a barrier to young men who could render good service as parish ministers but who feel no urge to embark upon the stern and dangerous business of being a prophet. Such a warning fails to take into account both the record of the centuries and the spirit of the youth of today. The times when the Church has been most vigorous in her assault upon the forces of evil and has, thereby, suffered severest persecution have been precisely the times when volunteers for her ministry have been most numerous. It is a significant fact that Timothy was recruited for the Christian ministry not at Athens, where Paul debated with the philosophers, nor at Corinth, where he lived in comparative security, but at Lystra, where he was stoned and dragged out of the city to die. The surest way for the Church to find enough men of the right quality to fill the ranks of her ministry is by the kind of courageous living that demonstrates that the gospel is to be practiced now.

We are thinking here, however, not simply of the initial call to the ministry, but of the summons that reaffirms itself, in various ways, through all the years of a man's life. The most secure basis for a dependable home life is for the husband and wife to keep on falling in love all over again. This ministry of ours is like that. Could there be a sadder or more depressing sight than a minister of Christ whose call has become a dim and receding memory, and whose service in his parish has slipped down to the dull level of a routine professionalism? The vigor and enthusiasm of youth will sometimes carry a man through the early part of his ministry without benefit of experiences that bring renewal of purpose and refreshing of soul. But when the years take their toll and a man thinks he has ceased climbing and looks ahead to what appears to be a gradually descending plateau, then it is that he needs a renewed call and a fresh commission. And God has it in his keeping to give such reassurances. Sometimes they come without heralds and from unexpected sources. After a long, hard climb up a steep slope, when the preacher is tempted to question whether the road leads anywhere, the way turns sharply, and there is disclosed the green valley and beyond it—the City of God. Moments like these, even if they do not come too frequently, can give a man strength and hope for the long days ahead. Phillips Brooks must have been at such a place when he said, "I pity the fellows who are not parsons."

In the Scripture it is recorded that "the gifts and the calling of God are without repentance." By this is meant, I suppose, that when God gives us something he does not become regretful and take it back. However this may be with respect to the call to the ministry, the fact remains that this high vocation can be invalidated on the human side by laziness, avoidable clumsiness, or the demons of envy, lust, and pride. On the other hand, the gift can be treasured and nurtured in such a way that it becomes increasingly real and life-releasing with the passing of the years. Thanks be to God for that valiant company of veterans who, in spite of failing physical energies, have never lost the glow and the glory of the hour when they knew that divine necessity had been laid upon them! They

18

bear a more potent witness for the Cross than they know. When Dr. John E. Godbey, a beloved preacher and teacher, came to his eighty-third birthday, someone asked him, "Doctor, if you had the privilege of making such a choice, which ten years of your long life would you prefer to live over again?" Without a moment's hesitation, the answer came back, "The next ten." The road goes on.

Effectiveness comes at a price

The second condition to a worthy ministry is *adequate preparation* for the exacting demands of a modern parish. There is something about us that gives us a sense of joy and release in doing the things which we know how to do well. We build up an attitude of resentment toward the things which we do awkwardly and with a disproportionate outlay of energy. This is the reason why many a preacher gets so little joy out of his work. He has never learned how to do it with a sense of ease and confidence. He began his ministry with false ideas and incomplete preparation. Each succeeding mistake becomes a part of the record and makes another error more nearly inevitable. During the first five years of his ministerial life the pattern of action was set, and since that time he has been moving in the groove of ineffectiveness. I am convinced, after an experience of ten years of observing the work of pastors, that there are many ministers who are achieving far below the level of their abilities simply because they have never learned how to do their work with competence and skill.

It is heretical, of course, to question whether we have made progress at this point since the proportion of pastors who have had advantage of seminary training has increased so greatly. But there is room for doubt. I would not be misunderstood at this point. I have the highest regard for the work that is being done by the seminaries. The young man looking to the ministry who does not secure the advantage of such training is robbing himself and the Church of his highest level of possible usefulness. There must be no retreat from this established fact. But it may as well be frankly recognized that our seminaries, with marginal exceptions, are not majoring in the business of training men for the pastorate. A large percentage of the graduates, including many of the most capable ones, leave the seminaries with the desire to become scholars and teachers and various kinds of specialists. On their day of graduation the pastorate with its routine demands does not loom large in their thought or plans. Gratitude should be recorded for progress in bringing to theological faculties, for full or for temporary assignment, men who embody the pastoral ideal at its best. But expectations for the immediate future need not be too hopeful.

And then there is the possibility that it is not the primary business of the seminaries to train men for the detailed work of the pastorage but rather to give them the broader understanding of theological learning out of which such a ministry can successfully and perennially grow. In the medical profession it is not assumed that a man is qualified to be a practicing physician simply because he has been graduated from a school of medicine. He must spend at least two years in an internship in a hospital under the guidance of older doctors before he is permitted to take the full responsibility for the healing of sick bodies. There was a time when a similar custom was followed in the major branches of the Protestant Church. That was the day of the junior pastorate. Perhaps our fathers were wiser than we are. When a young man entered the ministry in their day he was placed under the tutelage of an older preacher. With this senior pastor he traveled the circuit. As they rode together they talked about the problems which the preacher must deal with. At night the young man would read the older man's books. Together they went into the homes of the people. Together they had all kinds of experiences in helping people to be Christians. After a year of this kind of close comradeship the young preacher had absorbed enough of the spirit and methods of the older one to be able to venture out under his own direction. Some senior pastors were, of course, more gifted as teachers than others, but on the whole the body of ministerial tradition was remarkably well preserved by this method of transmittal.

Statistics have meaning

One of the peculiar perils of the ministry from which most other craftsmen are protected is the difficulty of making accurate report upon the results of the week's toil. The insurance salesman can add up his sales, the lawyer knows whether he has won or lost the verdict, the doctor can tell whether he has been able to keep his patient alive. Even the athlete writes a record which is preserved. It is a simple matter to find out how many hits, runs, and errors were made by any baseball player during his entire career with a major league. But with the minister it is different. So much that he deals with is in the realm of the intangible that statistics, it would appear, have little value. His work takes hold upon eternity and it is not to be expected that the results of his labors can be subjected to the categories of mundane achievements.

But, if we propose to be honest with ourselves and with our God-given vocation, we must remember that while some of the things which we do cannot be put down on statistical blanks, there are other things that can be so recorded. The preacher can never be sure of the degree to which his preaching incites his people to nobler living, but he can tell exactly how many hours he spends during the week in honest labor in his study. There is no way by which he can find out the extent to which his prayers were a factor in bringing people to an acquaintance with Christ. But he need not be in doubt as to the number of purposeful pastoral calls he has made, and the annual report requires that he find out how many people are attending the church school, and how many have stood at the altar of his church during the year to declare their allegiance to Christ. The degree to which the spirit of Christian stewardship has mastered the lives of his members will always remain something of a secret. But there are easy and direct methods by which it can be determined whether the financial obligations of his church are being met, whether the house of worship is being cared for or neglected, and to what extent the members of his church are providing for the affairs of the Kingdom with a worthy proportion of their income. Things that are visible are revealers of things that are invisible; therefore, statistics are not to be despised. "Arithmetic should not be banished," Bishop Edwin H. Hughes tells us, "because it condemns us. If we are doing good work, the more people we are helping the better the work." The conviction persists that there is an inseparable relationship between the things which are registered in the pastor's daily record of activities and the things which are recorded in heaven.

I know a layman who has cultivated the very annoying and disquieting habit of probing into church records, local and general. He seeks diligently to find the cause for certain trends in church life which the yearbooks reveal. In commenting on a recent compilation of statistics he said, "I have stated repeatedly, through the years, that in my studies of better-than-average churches and their church schools, I find that success seems to follow a minister from charge to charge six times out of seven. In only one out of seven local situations so studied have comparable results been maintained in the local church under successive pastorates." This research, which covers a period of many years, seems to point to the fact that some men have established in their ministry a pattern of success and others of failure. There are grounds for the belief that with the exception of a relatively small number of men who should never have entered the ministry at all, there is no reason why failure should be accepted as anything other than a challenge to the discovery of better methods and renewed enthusiasm. The fact that a man was well prepared for the demands of the pastoral ministry ten years ago does not necessarily mean that he is prepared today. The procession moves on. A wise teacher in seminary used to say to us, "My brethren, no man can hope to succeed in the Christian ministry unless he is willing to make a schoolboy of himself every day."

There can be little question that many pastors who have

moved into the postmeridian period of their ministry are following patterns of activity that are only fractionally productive. And it is not foreordained that it should be so. There is something that can be done about it. One of the most heartening discoveries of modern psychology is that the power to assimilate new ideas and to enter into new ways of living is not withdrawn with the passing of the half-century mark. In the realm of ministerial excellence it is possible for a man to be "born again" when his grand-children think he is old. Stirring books, summer conferences, correspondence courses, schools of evangelism, short courses in seminaries—all of these agencies, and others, hold out beckoning hands to the preacher who has become dissatisfied with a record that wavers between mediocrity and failure, and who believes that for the sake of God and man he ought to do better. There are tensions in life which blight and destroy; there are other tensions which, without depleting our energies, keep us stretching toward our highest possibilities. On this high ground we feel but poorly qualified to exhort each other, and if I should call for penitents in the light of this need for a new enduement of grace I would want to be the first to kneel at the altar.

"If I could get a chance at something big"

The third prerequisite to a productive and satisfying ministry is the ability to discover the extraordinary opportunity in the ordinary situation. I suspect it is failure at this point, more than at any other, that accounts for the fact that a considerable number of pastors lose the sense of thrill from their ministry after they pass the mid-period of their lives. It is a natural ambition—and one that should not be discouraged—for a young man to desire to come to the largest place in the Church for which his gifts and training have qualified him. There are certain statistical facts, however, that must be reckoned with. With ample allowance for anticipated growth, it is not likely that the ratio of the smaller churches to the larger ones will be greatly changed in this generation. It is a certainty as inexorable as the multiplication table that a large majority of pastors will always be serving in small churches.

Does this mean, then, that four out of five pastors must either be on the waiting list for a larger church to be vacated or become the victims of a sense of failure and defeat? Not at all. It simply means that we must develop a new appreciation of the distinctive possibilities of the small pastoral charge. Along with this shift of emphasis will come the recovery of a sense of the dignity and intrinsic worth of community life that is removed from the congested centers of population. Many Americans are beginning to believe that Arthur E. Morgan is correct when he insists that the small community has supplied the life-blood of civilization and that wherever its welfare is neglected the course of human progress is retarded. The god of bigness has dominated the greater part of the thinking and planning in American life for seventy-five years. It may be that one of the church's best ministries to this generation will be the rediscovery of the worth of the individual and of the indispensable place which the small community holds in the life of a democracy.

One of the hurtful results of a restless and discontented ministry is reflected in the brevity of pastoral tenure. In a day when community life has become more stable, the church it still attempting to operate, very largely, on the basis of a pioneer pattern of administration. The average length of pastorate in my own church is less than four years; with more than fifty per cent of pastors who move most frequently it is less than two years. The annual moving bill of these preachers in America is big enough to maintain an entire missionary colony for a year. My acquaintance with other Protestant bodies leads to the belief that their record at this point is substantially the same. How can there then be any depth of acquaintance or continuity of pastoral oversight when such nomadic customs prevail? It is not likely that we shall make great progress toward a more productive type of church life until the causes for these ministerial wanderings are found and corrected.

Recently I read a book called *Plainville, U.S.A.* by a trained sociologist who wrote under the pen name of James West. It is an intimate description of the ways in which people live together in a Midwestern town of sixty-five homes and a dozen stores. It might be noted that the portrayal of the place which the Church holds in the life of this community is not such as to increase one's pride in the contribution that Protestantism is making to our American culture. But the point of the book which impressed me most was the fact that the writer spent seventeen months in this town with the sole objective of getting acquainted with its people. He was not there to change anything or to reform anybody. He was there simply to find out what the people were thinking, how they were living, and by what processes they had come to be where they were. He was not ready to make even a partial report on his findings until he had lived in the town for almost a year and a half.

And yet I have known preachers who insisted that they could get quite well acquainted with their parishes in three weeks. It simply cannot be done, and the man who thinks that he has managed it has limited himself to superficials. The kind of relationships which are essential to the most enduring kind of pastoral service are not quickly established. They grow through the years. Doors into hearts and homes which do not open through six years will sometimes open during the seventh year, and pastors who have remained in the same parish for twenty years report that the twentieth year has witnessed the discovery of means of entrance into territory which had up to that time been forbiddingly marked "Keep off." All of this is, of course, based upon the assumption that the pastor will continue to grow. If that is not the case, then a single year is one year too long.

Still, a word of warning is needed by the pastor who stays for a long while in the same parish. He is surrounded by the subtle peril of conformity. He is faced by the constant danger of accepting things as they are. It is possible for a man to look at an unpainted church or an unholy community practice for so long a time that he becomes accustomed to it. The next deadly step is to tacitly assume that nothing can be done about it. It is good for a preacher to feel at home in his community but never too much at home. The chief advantage of a system which sent pastors to a different church every two or three years lay in the fact that a man of courage and resourcefulness was repeatedly going into a new community and bringing to pass needed reforms before he had been there long enough to discover that the old customs could not be altered. Now that we have come to the day of longer pastorates, this necessary tension between "things as they are" and "things as they ought to be" must be supplied by the conscience of a pastor who makes it his business to measure the progress of his people by the best that he has been able to find outside his parish and, more especially, by what he knows of God's will for individual and community life as Christ has revealed it.

The difficulty that is met in getting young men to go into unalluring fields of sevice has tempted us, at times, to the cynical feeling that they are losing the hardihood of the pioneer stock and are unwilling to face the privations of insecure and inconvenient living. A more careful reading of the facts will reveal that in most instances this is not the case. These men, we must remember, have wives to support and children to educate. And they have learned that the Church has sufficient material resources in her keeping to provide, if properly administered, a decent standard of living with reasonable conveniences for all her ministers. My observation is that men—capable and well trained— do not hesitate to go into uninviting and obscure places if they can have the assurance that they go there as the representatives of the Church and that the Church goes with them.

Some men are best suited by temperament and training for a ministry in the city. They should go to the city and stay. Other men, for like reasons, should go to the country and stay. With allowance for these exceptions there should always be a sufficient interchange of personnel and of points of view to keep each group informed of what the other is thinking and doing and to avoid the blight of a ministerial caste system. With the processes of decentralization already at work, and with the channels of intercommunication constantly enlarging, the essential unity of these two areas of the Church's life will become more and more apparent.

It would be a valuable contribution to the body of pastoral literature if a capable historian would write the story of the place the small parish has held in the development of the Christian Church. If he should limit himself to the more recent period, he might well begin with Kidderminster—and Richard Baxter. This English village where the besotted people were chiefly engaged in making carpets would scarcely have been chosen as the place for a historic ministry from which would emanate a personal force that would influence the course of Protestant thought and activity for three centuries.

Nearly two hundred years after Baxter's death Dean Stanley said, "There have been three or four parishes in England which have been raised by their pastors to a national, almost a world-wide fame. Of these the most conspicuous is Kidderminster: for Baxter without Kidderminster would have been but half himself; and Kidderminster without Baxter would have had nothing but its carpets."

Such a list would include the little town of Waldbach in Alsace, where John Frederick Oberlin, whom we have already mentioned, gave himself with unstinted generosity for more than half a century. So virile was his spirit that it recently reincarnated itself in the Oberlin Fellowship, which gives comradeship and encouragement to rural pastors of New England. Scotland would furnish notable examples of such creative parishes. There are highland manses with no house for neighbor, except the kirk, which have been occupied by ministers who have had the best training the seminaries in Edinburgh and Aberdeen could provide. And from these same manses have come stirring books that reveal a reach of scholarship not attained by men who are compelled to labor in the pressure of the crowd. And from these parishes there have gone into the cities a stream of youth so well grounded in the faith that they could not be shaken. Surely the list should include a certain country parish in Lincolnshire, Epworth by name. It was never a large parish, even with the "out-appointment" Wroote, nor particularly noted for the piety and generosity of its parishioners. But from that parsonage was released a torrent of spiritual force that has perceptibly lifted the moral temperature of the world.

And our own country has not been lacking in its share of praiseworthy examples of what can be done in a small parish if a man stays long enough, and prays and toils with sufficient faithfulness. Were it not for the peril of omission I could call the names of men of strength and vision who, with no sense of apology or self-pity, have given of themselves unstintingly in the service of small churches in congested cities, in little towns, in the open country. They have tarried and labored in the same place until something of their own nobler qualities has been written indelibly into the life of the community. To the man who has been mastered by the vast proportions of this ministry, and who has felt something of the majesty of the Kingdom which it seeks to establish, there are no small or unimportant places. He knows that people are there and resolves that the best he can provide for their nurture and growth shall be gladly and royally given.

Bishop Quayle used to insist that the tenth chapter of John's Gospel, where Jesus called himself the good shepherd, is the New Testament rescript of the Shepherd Psalm. And, indeed, the parallelism is close and intimate: "The Lord is my shepherd; I shall not want"; "I am the good shepherd, and know my sheep." "He maketh me to lie down in green pastures"; "He calleth his own sheep by name, and leadeth them out." "He restoreth my soul; he leadeth me in paths of righteousness"; "I am come that they might have life, and that they might have it more abundantly." But we must not allow the line of succession to stop there. Any man who is called of God to be a pastor, who has made and continues to make full preparation for his vocation, and who is giving all that he is and has that Christ may be known as the Lord of life—such a man is within the limits of truth and reverence when he says, "I am a good shepherd; I lay down my life for the sheep."

II

THE WORK OF AN EVANGELIST

PROLONGED SEARCH HAS BEEN MADE FOR TERMS TO CARRY the weight of the words "evangelist" and "evangelism" without certain unhappy connotations. But the quest has not been successful. There simply are no adequate substitutes for these words which have been through the centuries the verbal symbols of a creative force without which the Church could never have been born and apart from which it would quickly die. They are words of honorable parentage, they have been baptized with the fire of the Spirit, and they must not now be disclaimed.

I am not attempting here a definition of these words. Let each man arrive at his own definition. If he is interested in derivations, the search will send him to the Greek and Latin languages, where the root idea grows out of the concepts of good news of extraordinary importance. Following them from that beginning down through the years, he will feel the lift of an ever-widening stream that gives life to all that it touches. As he allows his imagination to picture what could happen in this day of confusion if the life-giving power which these words signify should be fully released, there will rise before him the spires of the City of God. He may be sure that after he has made his definition with all possible breadth and inclusiveness, it will still not be large enough and, if he is a growing preacher, it will be larger tomorrow.

If in the light of the truest definition he can form, a man should say, "But I am not an evangelist," it would mean that he could not be a pastor unless he were willing to be a parasite. There can be no congregation of Christians in any century or on any continent until through the labors and prayers of evangelists the people to constitute that congregation have been brought into the fellowship of Christ. But no man who has been called into this ministry will seriously make this statement of himself. He may insist that he has no proficiency in the use of methods which others employ with success. Or he may say that this part of his work is not easy for him. It rarely is. But he cannot mean that he does not regard the enlisting of followers of Christ as a part of his commission as a minister. It would be of no consequence for us to talk about applying the gospel to the social problems of the day if there were no individual Christians and no congregations of Christians through whom the application could be made.

The perils of an incomplete gospel

What, then, are some of the things that we need to set before us as we seek to do the work of evangelists? We can begin with the fact that we need a new conception of *the inclusiveness of the gospel*. We have the doctrinal framework for it—no one will question that. And we have the phraseology. But do we have the reality of it? To put the matter more directly, is it the usual thing for a pastor to recognize that he and the members of his congregation are responsible for winning to Christian discipleship every person in his parish who does not already belong to the Church? Are we not in grave danger of becoming a party

33

to an unholy truce with the forces of irreligion by which we say, "If you won't trouble us, we won't trouble you?" Our constant peril is that we shall divide the people into two classes—those who "belong" to us and those who do not. And the next step is to lose interest in those who are outside of our circle, with the exception of those who would fit in gracefully. When that day comes, the nerve of a vital evangelism is cut and we settle down to a comfortable parochialism—and death.

As one means of keeping the terms of his commission before him, a pastor should ask himself at least once each month, "Is there any sufficient reason why even one person in my parish should not be a Christian?" He should then set before himself another question. "What kind of a community would this be if everybody in it were a Christian?" Here the image begins to blur, and doubt creeps in as to whether anybody would want to live there. If everybody in a community were like some church members we have known, we are quite certain that life there would be stale, drab, and uninteresting. This is the basis for the rather common though unconfessed feeling that, although it ought not to get out of control, a little bit of wickedness is a good thing to have around as a means of giving color and zest to living. All of which means that we have not yet arrived at a full-grown interpretation of what Christianity really is.

There is heresy abroad which insinuates that to be a Christian one must surrender something of his individuality and become a kind of colorless stereotype. This would mean that the main business of Christianity is to flatten humanity to a dead-level of uniformity in thought and action. No lie of the devil was ever falser. It is in Christ that individual personality is lifted to its highest level of distinctiveness. We never become our real selves until we find them in him. Separated from his truth, however it may have been released, humanity slips down to the sordid plane of bestiality—and lower. One of the paradoxes of our faith is that the more like Christ we become the greater are our individual differences. Professor C. S. Lewis of Oxford has given us many fresh and bold insights into the gospel. The one that helps us here is his parable of light in the physical world. He says that if people had always lived in darkness they would imagine that if they should come into the light they would all reflect the same light and would, therefore, all look alike. The fact is, the light would reveal how different they are.

Genuine goodness is never colorless, and the variations of it are infinite. Sinful living can never be other than rigidly restricted, and its only means of making itself attractive is to use for a mask the qualities which belong to goodness. Any liquor advertisement will illustrate what I mean. The point of emphasis here is that community life with Christ in control instead of being drab and monotonous would be rich and varied beyond anything we have known. Individual gifts and talents that had never been suspected would be discovered and new ways of glorifying God and of enriching human life would continually be brought into action.

All of this is based upon the assumption that the ideal of living, individual and social, which the Church fosters is expansive enough to keep life from becoming narrow and sterile. But is this the case? At times, in a mood of discouragement, we raise the question, "Why aren't more people being converted? Why is the progress of the Church so painfully slow?" Does it ever occur to us that the growth of the Church may be altogether as rapid as its breadth of spirit warrants; that for converts to be won in great numbers on the basis of its present imperfections would not be in the interest of the Kingdom's advance but rather an added barrier to its coming? It follows that the evangelistic obligation requires the Church to continue its self-examination in the light of the standard which Christ has set. A church that has serious hopes of making conquest of the world must have a conception of the gospel which is not only big enough to include everybody but spacious enough to provide for all of the legitimate hungers of mankind.

The eternal hunger for God

Martin Luther defined faith as "a rejoicing confidence that we have a merciful God." A second basic requirement for a virile evangelism today is *the recovery of such a faith,* wherever it has grown dim. With this recovery will come the renewal of the conviction that Christ has power to change human life—to lift man to the plane of living where God intended he should be. In all our present uncertainty and confusion there is one fact which stands out like a beacon light: the human heart is eternally hungry for God. Through all of man's paganism and secularism and materialism, the God who made him for Himself will not allow him to be other than restless until he find rest in the Eternal.

One of the strange and puzzling things about man is

that this instinctive hunger could have found so many ways of becoming perverted. But it never completely dies. It seems quite evident from the record which the race has written during the last five or six thousand years that the human heart is so constructed that it will not remain empty. When a satisfying faith in God is excluded, something else comes in to take its place. One of these substitutes is superstition. The relationship between religion and superstition is very close. The root in the Greek language is identical. These two forms of the soul's outreach after God, the true and the false, spring from the same basic hunger. Superstition is the piteous wail of a starving soul. Most Americans are inclined to be proud of an attitude of realism which is the product of scientific enlightment. The truth of it is that this boasted devotion to the uniformity of natural law is quite superficial. It is estimated that there are in America more than eighty thousand fortunetellers, crystal-gazers, palm readers, spiritualist mediums, astrologers and soothsayers of various kinds, who are retained at an annual cost of nearly a third of a billion dollars. Dr. Halford E. Luccock once remarked that when a man reels back from a great faith, he usually falls into a grouch, a mood of despair, or a convenient superstition. Whatever may be said for the others, superstition is unquestionably having its field day.

Another evidence of this hunger in America is found in the rapid growth of certain religious sects which have developed since the beginning of the century. Dr. Marcus Bach estimates that these groups now have fifteen million direct or indirect adherents. He believes that they are growing at a rate of a million every five years, half of the converts coming from the churches and the other half from the ranks of those who are overlooked by the churches. After every possible allowance has been made for various types of abnormal psychology, the fact remains that a vast number of people in America are finding in those little-known sects an answer to their religious hungers which they had not found elsewhere. After describing the beliefs and practices of eight of these sects, Dr. Bach writes in his book *They Have Found a Faith:* The "democracy of Protestant-ism, which allowed every man to become his own priest, made no provision for the people who want to be told pre-cisely what to believe and exactly how to believe it. They go, therefore, where they can find prescribed techniques. In almost every modern movement the ideal of a social religion is subordinated to an emphasis on the individual. Every seeker is convinced that there is something within him to which a direct revelation of God can appeal. Then follows a continual sense of wonder at his own spiritual de-velopment. The commonest blessings suddenly become 'gifts from God.' In return for these he is attached by a new allegiance of service to the organization. The smaller the group, the greater his loyalty." [1]

Church history makes it plain that heresies are frag-mentary interpretations of the truth which spring up in response to legitimate hungers of the soul which the Church has neglected. It is possible to find many defective elements in most of these marginal religious sects—intolerance, overemotionalism, obscurantism, by-passing of the ethical demands of life. But it is wiser to recognize their growth as evidence of two facts that must be reckoned with. The

[1] *They Have Found a Faith* (Bobbs-Merrill Co., 1946), p. 293.

first is a failure on the part of the major Protestant denominations to maintain a warmth of inner assurance
which satisfies the hunger of those whose approach to religion is not primarily intellectual. The second is the failure to provide adequately for the religious instruction and
pastoral oversight of the "unshepherded multitudes" who
because of economic insecurity or social maladjustment
reach out eager hands for something that will endure. A
partial faith can be very confident and very dynamic. But
it is always under the peril of disillusionment which comes
in with the light. There is no justification for assuming that
the religious choice of America must be between a sterile
liberalism and an irresponsible fanaticism. The major problem continues to be exactly where Wesley found it two
centuries ago: "To unite these two, so long divided: learning and vital piety." A purified and reinvigorated Protestantism will set itself to the consummation of such a union.

Still another example of the man's instinctive faith in a
Power higher than himself is his amazing tendency to make
a god of the state and bow down and worship it. Men have
given to this false deity a devotion which only God has the
right to require. The extent of this idolatry would be beyond our belief if it had not been witnessed in our own
generation. Even more unbelievable than this delusion is
the tendency to deify a man. The hunger of the human
heart for the personal element in religion probably accounts for this trend. With characteristic American optimism and self-confidence we say, "But it couldn't happen
here." A generation ago it was believed that it could not
happen in Europe. Two generations ago progressive leaders
in Japan thought it could not happen there. The stark truth

is that if, for a single generation, the light of the gospel should be withheld and the Church should turn its back upon its obligations to be the conscience of the nation, it is folly to predict what could or could not happen here. The man who undertakes the business of evangelism— preacher or layman—as if it were merely a matter of securing a few members for the Church has failed utterly to understand the crucial importance of his commission. The recruits which such a man might secure would either drop out of the ranks quickly or they would be astonished when they discovered what the Church is actually undertaking to do.

Secondhand experience is not sufficient

Out of this confusion of tongues and this fierce competition for the souls of men there emerges one central truth: if the Christian religion is to demand and secure men's deepest loyalties it must speak again with an authority that is born of a *firsthand contact with God*. This is another way of saying that the Christian doctrine of conversion, which for two generations has been in grave danger of complete neglect, must be restored to its rightful place in the thought and experiences of the Church. Until somewhere near the beginning of the present century the usual method of joining the Church in the larger Protestant bodies in America was through a conversion experience. In all probability the proportion of crisis conversions, even at that time, was not as great as some have estimated, but it was still the generally accepted way of entering the Kingdom. With the increased emphasis upon the "gradual development" concept of life and the vigorous promotion of the educational approach to religious experience, the ratio shifted rapidly. So much so that nearly twenty years ago Dr. Elmer T. Clark, on the basis of a widely representative study, reported that "more than ninety percent of the persons who today call themselves religious have never undergone any such experience, but became religious through a process of growth, attended in certain cases by the general ferment of adolescence and slight emotional stirring of a religious nature." [2] What such a study would reveal today is a matter of speculation but it is quite certain that the percentage of church members who are aware of any moment in their lives when God made himself known to them in any direct way has not increased.

A century ago Horace Bushnell rebelled against a rigid and distorted doctrine of conversion and announced as his major thesis "that the child is to grow up a Christian, and never know himself as being otherwise." There can be no dissent from the fact that this interpretation of the child's relation to the Kingdom was needed in that day—and in this day. But an unfortunate consequence of the reversal of emphasis is that for the past thirty years the evangelistic methods of the Protestant churches have been so largely confined to this conception of religious development that there has been a progressive failure to make adequate provision for the large element of the people who will never be brought into the Kingdom in any other manner than through a definite crisis conversion. And we must not lose sight of the fact that there are from twenty to twenty-five million children and young people in America who are growing up in spiritual illiteracy. What possibility

[2] *Psychology of Christian Experience.*

41

is there for them to "grow up as Christians"? These figures do not take into account the millions who have already reached adulthood nor the youth who have had an irregular kind of religious teaching but have not made commitment of their lives to Christ. This is no suggestion for relaxation in the use of all of the agencies which Christian education has provided for the uninterrupted spiritual nurture of the child. Many a prodigal never returns, and when he does he always leaves something in the far country. But it is a plea for the fuller use of a means of rescuing broken humanity that holds for many people their only hope of release from the bondage of sin.

Our fellow Christians in England, where the Church is hard pressed for her very life, have declared their faith with respect to the place that must be given to conversion. A commission on evangelism appointed by the archbishops of Canterbury and York made recommendations to the Church of England two years ago in a report entitled "Towards the Conversion of England." These fifty representatives of a church which is usually regarded as being predominantly liturgical were frankly outspoken in their conviction that something more than outward ceremonial is required. "The aim of evangelism," says this commission, "is conversion. Conversion is the reorientation of life from self to God through Christ Jesus. Conversion may be sudden: a revolutionary experience, like a revealing flash of lightning, which enables the convert to commemorate a spiritual birthday. Or conversion may be gradual: an evolutionary development, like the dawn of day, or the miracle of the harvest field. But whether sudden or gradual, it is the birthright of every child of God to be converted, or, in St. Paul's phrase, to 'be *alive* unto God in Jesus Christ our Lord! ' Short of this there is no stopping place for the evangelist, no sure resting place for the convert." [3]

William James defined conversion as "the process, gradual or sudden, by which a self, hitherto divided and consciously wrong, inferior and unhappy, becomes unified and consciously right, superior and happy." These were familiar terms at the beginning of the century: "divided . . . consciously wrong . . . inferior . . . unhappy." But what new and poignant meanings they have acquired through these years while the psychologists and psychiatrists probed, with the persistence of sleuths, into the depths of this mysterious thing that we call the human mind! But, after all, Christians had no cause to be shocked by what has been discovered. At the very beginning of our era a man laid bare his soul and told us something of the base and corrupt things he found there:

"The law is spiritual; but I am carnal, sold under sin. I do not understand my own actions. I do not do what I really desire, but I do the very thing I hate. . . . I delight in the law of God, in my inmost self, but I see in my body another law at war with the law of my mind and making me captive to the law of sin which dwells in my body."

And this man tells us of the fierce struggle that went on within his soul until he was beaten down to a confession of hopeless defeat. And then an amazing victory came— not won so much as given. "For the law of the Spirit of life in Christ Jesus made me free from the law of sin and

[3] *Towards the Conversion of England,* The Press and Publications Board of the Church Assembly (Westminster) p. 36.

death.'" "Unified . . . consciously right . . . superior . . . happy."

And this power by which defeat is turned into victory is in reach today. It is astonishing that, in the presence of such urgent need of it, the Church has not said more about it. But after all, this is one of the facts of the gospel that has most force when it is demonstrated rather than discussed. The Church needs to put increased vigor into her program of Christian education. Yes! It must be made perfectly clear that there is no standardized method of entering the Kingdom. Certainly! But this is not enough. Through emphasis in preaching and teaching upon the Christian doctrine of conversion, by maintaining in the life of his church an atmosphere of expectancy, and by providing a favorable setting in public and private worship, the pastor can make it possible for some of the people of his parish to find their way to God through an experience of spiritual rebirth who will not find it in any other way.

"Of such is the Kingdom"

Sound evangelistic methods are essential. Many a pastor has failed to do the work of an evangelist not because he was lacking in willingness or was in doubt about God's forgiving grace but because he did not know how to take hold. During a recent year of evangelistic emphasis in one of the larger denominations the tides of enthusiastic effort ran deep and strong. Even with this special incentive there were more than nine hundred pastors of this denomination who reported not a single addition to their churches on confession of faith for the entire year. We cannot believe that there were this many pastors who were in parishes where there were no unconverted people or who just did not care. The answer in most of these cases is that these men had never learned how to introduce people to Christ.

This is not the place for a detailed discussion of methods. I shall mention, for brief comment, the three forms of evangelism which have always been and will continue to be the major channels through which the urge to reach people with the Christian good news will express itself.

The logical place to begin is with the church school. The children of the Church belong to us, and God will not hold us guiltless if we allow them to wander away without being brought to the place of decision in terms of Christian discipleship. With from sixty to eighty per cent of the accessions to the Church coming through the church school, it might be assumed that a corresponding proportion of the pastor's attention would be given to this form of evangelism. This, however, is not the case in most instances. Church-school evangelism has been in operation long enough to have resulted in the entrance of a substantial majority of the members who are now in the churches through that method. The fact that only thirty-five per cent of Protestant church members attend the worship service with any degree of regularity and only fifty per cent contribute to the financial support of the Church is to be attributed largely to the lax and superficial methods by which they have been brought into church membership.

A minimum requirement for the evangelism of children and youth will involve at least the following five factors.

First, a meeting as soon as possible after New Year's Day with the church-school teachers of the junior department and youth division. At this meeting the evangelistic opportunity of the church-school teacher will be fully discussed and a calendar of procedure will be agreed upon by which each class will be brought to a clear understanding of what is involved in making a commitment of life to Christ. Second, a decision-day service with each age group. No other service of the year will require more careful preparation on the part of the pastor. The service should be conducted in such a way that decisions can be on the basis of personal choice and not as the result of undue group influence. In many cases the decision for Christ will already have been made under the leadership of teachers or parents. The decision day service will be the opportunity for a public expression of the decision. Third, a training class with a sufficient number of sessions to give to the preparatory members an understanding of the meaning of church membership in keeping with their age and development. There can be no adequate substitute for the pastor's leadership of this group, even in the largest churches, and no other investment of time will be more rewarding. During this period of training, every effort should be made to enlist the co-operation of parents in the religious nurture of the children. Fourth, a reception service so impressive that it cannot easily be forgotten. It is probably wise to limit the reception of members at this service to the children and youth, and to their parents who are ready to join. Fifth, a suitable recognition of new members who have come through the training class in at least one service following the reception service.

But church-school evangelism is not enough. This is true for two reasons. First, there is too large a proportion of our American people who are not being reached by the church school and too large a number of those who are reached who leave the church school without having made the commitment of their lives to Christ. Second, the decisions which determine the religious atmosphere in which children must grow up are made almost entirely by adults. Dr. H. Shelton Smith faces us with a fact of history when he writes, "The Church should remember that great periods of religious rebirth have not emerged as the result of child-nurture. Religion has always come alive in the adult conciousness, and has usually involved a break with the religion inherited in childhood." He then goes on to say, "The inference to be drawn from this fact is not that the Church should renounce the function of Christian nurture. On the contrary, to the fullest possible extent the Church should share its life and faith with the young. This is a basic and continuing task of the Church. Nevertheless, the Church must not surrender to the illusion that child-nature, in itself, will rekindle the fire of life and faith in the Christian community. For the religion of the child will usually be a relatively pale edition of the faith of the older generation. This means that unless the faith comes alive in the soul of some mature individual or group religious vitality may be expected to decline in modern culture." [4] Not less attention but more must be given to bringing the children to Christ that life may be saved rather than salvaged. But there must also be a fuller realization that if the Church is in earnest about chang-

[4] *Faith and Nurture* (Charles Scribner's Sons, 1941), pp. 102-4.

ing the currents of thought and conduct, it must direct its efforts to the conversion of adults.

"He brought him to Jesus"

What are the means by which this can be done? The first is personal evangelism. The form which this method is taking just now with greatest effectiveness is visitation evangelism. It has been hailed as the heaven-sent answer to the problem of reaching people with the Christian gospel just at the time when the older forms of evangelism are becoming less effective. It has been criticized as being superficial in its method and transitory in its results. Depending upon the attitude and understanding in which it is undertaken, it may be either of these. If it is allowed to drop to the level of a high-pressure campaign for new members without regard to the deeper implications of Christian discipleship, the increase in numbers will be secured at the cost of bringing people into the Church on the basis of an unworthy understanding of the nature of this fellowship and of cheapening the conception of church membership for the entire congregation.

This method of evangelism has certain inherent qualities which assure its permanence. First, it has the advantage of having been thoroughly tested. It is as old as the Christian religion—indeed, it is as deeply fixed in human nature as the impulse to tell another of an amazing discovery. It is as natural and spontaneous as the procedure expressed by an old hymn, "Let me commend my Saviour to you." Second, it brings the layman into active participation instead of leaving him in the position of a spectator. One of the most hurtful tendencies from which evangelism has suffered is the disposition to make it the exclusive business of the ministry. Such an attitude is contrary to the spirit of the New Testament and certainly has no place in the Protestant interpretation of lay responsibility. The third advantage is that it assures to every member who comes into the fellowship of the Church by this method a vital contact with the congregation through the person or persons who helped to lead him to the commitment. Personal ties of this nature solve the problem of assimilation and help to bind the congregation into a living unity. It is not likely that more than a tenth of the adult members of a congregation will be fitted for the exacting requirements of personal evangelism. This does not mean that the other nine-tenths have no responsibility for maintaining in the church a spirit of understanding Christian fellowship which is the atmosphere of normal development. It is scarcely necessary to say that it should be the unfailing practice for the pastor or a dependable staff worker to have an unhurried interview, prior to the service of reception, with every person who asks to be received into the Church.

Mass evangelistic service

What use can be made today of the evangelistic mission —the modern successor to the old-fashioned revival? Some men tell us, quite emphatically, that the day for this type of evangelism has passed and may as well be forgotten. There can be no doubt that this means of winning converts, which has held so prominent a place in the growth of the Church in America, has largely fallen into disuse and in some quarters into disrepute. Whether or not we shall see again the kind of mass evangelism that is associated with the names of Dwight L. Moody, Billy Sunday, and Gipsy Smith is a question that the future must answer. To give a negative reply on the ground that modern man has become enlightened and sophisticated and, therefore, not amenable to group pressure, would be to disregard the fact that mass movements on a national scale have repeatedly occurred in the generation to which we belong. It would be strange, indeed, if at the very time when the techniques of group and mass psychology are being employed to distort and debauch men's minds, the Church should decide that they are not to be used as a means of bringing men to the decision which their deeper nature demands.

The question we are directly concerned with here is, "What use can the pastor make of this type of evangelism in his own church?" I am thinking specifically of the plan by which a period of from eight to fifteen days is observed annually as a time of evangelistic emphasis with one or two services daily in which the preaching is done by the pastor of the congregation or a visiting pastor. Where two or more churches work co-operatively in such a mission, the area of contact with the community is greatly enlarged. Instead of discussing the evangelistic mission in terms of its maximum possibilities, I prefer to begin on the solid ground of what any pastor who is willing to undertake it with earnestness and enthusiasm may be sure of accomplishing. First, it gives an opportunity for presenting, in a consecutive manner, certain areas of Christian truth that are vitally related to present-day living. Biblical and doctrinal illiteracy on the part of the average church member should be no occasion for surprise to those who are familiar with our inadequate system of instruction. This condition can be changed only by the diligent and continuous effort of pastors who believe that it really matters. Second, a definite part of each evening service should be used, under the direction of a capable song leader, for singing familiar hymns and learning new ones. The congregation's participation in this part of the worship service could be greatly increased by this kind of training for which there is not sufficient time on Sunday morning. Third, it makes possible the continuity of impression upon the consciences of persons who need to make crucial decisions. Conversions occur most frequently in the presence of a spiritual temperature which cannot be reached when services are separated by an intervening week. Fourth, it can be used to give meaning and validity to other methods of evangelism. Church-school evangelism and personal evangelism have a tendency to sink to the level of techniques for securing new members for an organization when they become separated from the dynamic and prophetic elements of the Christian imperative.

These are some of the assured values that will come from the evangelistic mission. And beyond them no limit can be fixed as to the good results that may come from this method of evangelism. When a pastor and his congregation make adequate preparation for such a special effort and enter into it with a spirit of eager confidence, the unexpected always happens. The miracle of grace will be wrought in the life of an individual or a home that was outside the area of immediate expectations and it will be demonstrated that when a congregation gives evidence of concern for the spiritual welfare of the people, the convicting and converting power of the gospel will manifest itself again.

The three methods stand together in a vitally related trilogy—church-school evangelism, personal evangelism, public evangelism—and we are not called upon to say which of the three is greatest.

"A new creation"

The *Revised Standard Version of the New Testament* has set thousands of people to reading the Book again with new zest. We never seem to be able to get from this living record all that it has to say to us. In the Book of Acts a statement which I had read many times came to life with a vividness of meaning which I had not felt before. Only a few words are different from the older versions, but these words became windows through which I looked at a scene for the first time. Three men are standing together, surrounded by an excited, gesticulating throng, some of whom are in places of high authority. It is easy to see that the mob is restrained in its hostility toward the men by some strange fact which it cannot account for. Here is the descriptive word picture, "But seeing the man that had been healed standing beside them, they had nothing to say in opposition." A man who until a few hours before had been a community burden is now able to stand on his own feet beside the men who have brought to him the healing word. However bitter may be the antagonism of the religious leaders to this new power, the lame man has been made to walk, and there really is nothing to be said in opposition.

The reality which stands as the gospel's chief credential is the fact that it can change human nature. Men and women for whom life had no hope because it had no meaning have found that Christ is the Way; personalities that had fallen into discordant fragments have been brought together around a center which is powerful enough to hold them in unity; slaves to vicious habits have been set free; families that were breaking on the rocks of selfishness and unfaithfulness have been guided into new channels; the moral and spiritual levels of whole communities have been raised; ideals which determine the course of a nation's life have been changed. So long as there stands beside us the man who has been healed, hope will not die and faith will continue to make its affirmation that a new world is within our reach.

III

FOR BUILDING UP
THE BODY OF CHRIST

"This is my parish." what a feeling of pride and of high responsibility comes to the pastor when he says these words for the first time! He is on territory that has been committed to his oversight and care. Living within its borders are people whom he has never met but who are soon to become a part of his life. In a very real sense they are his people. He is about to begin an association which in readiness of acceptance and closeness of bonds is without parallel among human relationships. The household goods have been unpacked; he has examined the church building in which the congregation worships; he has discovered the boundaries of his parish; the first worship service—the best place for the initial meeting with his people—has been held. And now he begins the process of getting acquainted with his congregation. This is an undertaking that will never be completed. However small the parish, there is never time enough for the pastor to become fully acquainted with all of his people. On the last day of his longest pastorate there will be areas of mystery about many of these lives which he has not been able to penetrate. How could it be otherwise since so many of them are mysteries to themselves? If in the seminary he has acquired the idea that people can be classified into four or five convenient

54

categories, that mistaken notion is soon laid aside. No two of these people are alike. Each is a distinct personality who recognizes himself as such and has in his mind a definite picture, correct or incorrect, of the kind of individual he is.

Why is he here?

After the preliminary survey of his parish has been made, he sits down to take stock of himself and of his obligation. Why, exactly, is he here? What is he to do? The teacher, the plumber, the doctor, and the groceryman know precisely what is expected of them. There are definite standards by which they can determine whether they are succeeding or failing. In the average parish there are certain people who know, unmistakably, what the pastor is to do and some of them will probably inform him without the formality of his asking. But do they really know?

The man who speaks for God must not forget the long procession of his spiritual ancestry. The very reason for his being grows out of the fact that when man turns away from God the light that is in him becomes darkness and life grows sordid and bestial. The resources of nature which God intended for his welfare are either wantonly wasted or converted into poisons for his own body and instruments of destruction for his neighbors. Instead of living with his fellow man in peace and good will, he sinks to the level of savage fighting more brutally destructive than that of the beasts of the jungle. In the wake of murder and rape and warfare come famine and disease. Mothers hold their starving babies to their breasts, and men curse the fact that they were born. Human frailty is overborne, and the burden of life becomes intolerable. In desperation and out of the blackness of despair man cries for help to whatever higher Power he believes in, and God, in his mercy, sends a man to speak for him. Sometimes this man is received, sometimes he is rejected; but rejected or received, he publishes his message, and light begins to dawn, and man begins again the long, slow climb toward God.

All of this seems remote from the quiet life of a pastor who lives in a comfortable parsonage in the security of an American village. But the line of succession is unbroken. If he and his comrades should relax their vigilance for a single year, the beast which always prowls hopefully at the edge of the circle of light would crouch for the death leap. The nearest approach to an answer to the question, "Why is this man here?" is this: "He is here to make people aware of God." His presence in the community is evidence that there are hungers in human life that cannot be satisfied with material prosperity. He represents life's ultimate reality without which all other values, material and spiritual, become cheap and insecure. The pastor's mission is indispensable.

"I was glad when they said unto me"

If this is his mission, what are the means within his reach for fulfilling it? How can he lead the people of his parish from where they are to the place where God wants them to be—the place where, in their finer moods, they themselves want to be? He will probably decide that the most logical place to take hold is at the point of the service of worship. Emerson said, "We descend to meet." This can be sadly— even tragically—true. A vast amount of meeting in our day is at a level which requires the leaving behind of the finer ideals and sometimes of reason itself. Anyone who has ever seen a mob in action has witnessed something that is ugly and bestial. A group that a little while before had consisted of separate individuals, each thinking and acting for himself, has been fused into a corporate unit. It behaves with the co-ordination of an individual and is motivated by depraved passions that not even the basest individual of the crowd would have surrendered to if he had been left to act alone. A mob is formed by people who have descended to meet.

It is also true that we ascend to meet. The call of God's people through the centuries has been, "Let us go up to the house of the Lord." The difference between a mob and an orderly assembly for worship is that one is dominated by its lowest instincts, which are incited by what the New Testament calls, "the spiritual hosts of wickedness"; the other is controlled by its highest tendencies, which are enlarged and inspired by the Spirit of God. It does not require a mystical type of mind to feel the uplift that comes from an hour of corporate worship. The hymns, the Scripture, the prayer, the fellowship—these together have the power to lift a man above the petty isolations of selfishness, to make him aware that he is a part of the marching procession of God's people, and to prepare him for the call to nobler living which the sermon ought always to give.

The church member who becomes careless and irregular in his habits of public worship is detaching himself from one of the most dependable sources of strength for living. Freedom of worship to many an American means freedom not to worship. It must be confessed that many of the practices of the average Protestant church school train the

57

children and youth away from established habits of congregational worship rather than toward them. The answer to this problem must be found if the worship habits of church members are to be better tomorrow than they are today. The layman will do well to go to the service of worship whether he likes it or not. A certain degree of discipline is as essential for spiritual growth as it is for physical health. But if a man finds it necessary always to compel himself to go to church as a matter of duty, either something is seriously wrong with the service, or this man has never been taught to appreciate the meaning and value of corporate worship.

A word is in order here about the downward pull of empty pews. No one has attempted, so far as I know, to calculate the depressive weight of vacant seats upon a service of worship. When seventy-five people are present at the regular hour of worship in a sanctuary that was designed for six hundred, an atmosphere of unfulfilled expectation is inescapable even though it may not be fully recognized by either the preacher or the people. It is the principle of the vacant place at the dinner table. Part of the fault lies in the fact that too many sanctuaries were built for special occasions rather than for the ordinary service. Surely this mistake will not be repeated in the days of new church buildings. Better to have a church overcrowded on special occasions or to repeat the service than to have great areas of empty pews at regular services. Good plans of reconstruction have, in some instances, reduced the size of sanctuaries and have added needed space for the Church school.

But the burden of responsibility for this situation is not

so much in the building as in the church members. This is not the place to attempt to locate the cause for Protestant laxity at the point of church attendance. But it must be said that no obligation of the pastor is more important than building a worshiping congregation. He will do this in two ways: first, by using all of the teaching facilities of the church to inculcate individual habits of public worship and, second, by making the service of worship more meaningful and attractive.

When the pastor comes to the arranging of the worship service he will find, whether he recognizes it or not, that the priest and the prophet within him contend for the dominant place. Indeed, this conflict will develop at various points all through his ministry. If the breadth of his calling is properly understood he will know that he is to be both priest and prophet. Every minister should study his own nature to discover the direction of his most vigorous trend and should set himself to the task of maintaining the proper balance between these two elements of a complete ministry. The needs of the people require both expressions of God's truth and it would be a misfortune for a congregation to have as pastor, for any considerable period of time, a man who lacked either of them.

However thoroughly the Protestant pastor may disavow the sacerdotal conception of his ministry, there will always be a sense in which he mediates between God and the congregation. It cannot be otherwise. In a day when the meaning of symbolism is being more fully appreciated in the Protestant church, why should there not be a fuller recognition of this personal symbolism? This is to be expected in a religion which has for its central reality the fact that "the Word became flesh and dwelt among us." The question then is simply whether the pastor will be a good priest or a careless, ineffective one. The choice of the hymns, the preparation for the pastoral prayer, the renewal of familiarity with the passage of Scripture to be read, the understanding with the choir concerning the special music and the choral responses—these are matters that must not be neglected nor trusted to the inspiration of the moment. And they are not to be regarded as elements of the service in preparation for the sermon but as divinely ordained means by which the worshiping congregation may be made more sure of God. The order of worship which has been established is not to be treated lightly. One of the conditions of a satisfactory worship experience is a knowledge of the order of service which enables the worshiper to devote his attention to the materials in use without constantly wondering what will come next. This kind of familiarity is not possible where the worship customs of the congregation are manipulated to suit the individual whims of each succeeding pastor. Most orders of service are sufficiently flexible to make allowance for special features without disrupting the basic pattern of adoration, confession, affirmation, and dedication. By the very manner in which he administers the sacraments of baptism and Holy Communion, the pastor will reveal to his congregation whether he believes that they stand for something that is ultimately real or are traditional exercises whose only value is in their psychological suggestiveness. The meaning and importance with which he interprets them will almost certainly be accepted by the congregation. The wedding ceremony and the funeral service are not simply occasions in which the presence of a minister has become a conventional custom. They are distinctive opportunities for allowing the light of Christian faith to illumine man's experience of joy and sorrow. Without descending to the level of a distasteful informality, it is possible for a pastor to reveal in these impressionable moments the reality of the bond between the human and the divine—between man and God.

The high place of preaching

The prophetic element of the Christian ministry has its best opportunity of expression in the sermon. What place in the service of worship is to be given to preaching? In the Protestant Church the answer to this question has had wide variations. There was a time when the sermon was regarded as the crowning glory of public worship with the other elements of the service having value only as a means of providing the proper setting for this central event. In the endeavor to recapture the magic of pulpit orators who have held great congregations spellbound there has been a temptation in Protestantism to make a fetish of the sermon and to believe that "great preaching" will provide sufficient warrant for the neglect of all other duties that are related to the pastoral ministry. In more recent times there has been a tendency among younger ministers to think of the sermon as an unwelcome chore to be disposed of as the price of administering an elaborate ritual or of getting to the more important business of personal counseling and social engineering. The correct answer is not found in either of these extremes.

The truest appraisal of the sermon's place in the service

of worship comes with understanding that it is not a thing separate and apart but is vitally related to the service as a whole. It is for this reason that the best preaching will always be done by pastors rather than by "occasional" preachers. The sermon is not a work of art to be wrought out in the secluded isolation of a pastor's study and brought in on Sunday morning to be admired for its literary excellence and its entertaining qualities. A sermon is a sincere and honest effort to bring a full measure of the resources of the Christian gospel into the areas of life where problems are perplexing and burdens are heavy. By this I do not mean that every sermon must begin with a statement of the problem or a description of the burden. "Life-situation preaching" can become as stereotyped and hackneyed as an older type of preaching which began in the stratosphere and never managed to connect with anything remotely related to everyday problems. When a man comes to church on Sunday morning worried about how he is to get enough money together to pay the note which falls due on Friday, it is not at all certain that the best way for the sermon to help him is by beginning with a description of his plight. That procedure, by centering his attention upon himself, could hurt rather than help. It may be that the best way to begin is by opening the way into a great truth that lifts the skies of the man's life so that he can stand erect in the confidence that he can count on God's help in working out his problem. But the plea that is here made is that, regardless of its point of beginning, no discourse qualifies as Christian preaching until it holds in proper relation the two poles of creative tension

—the reality of human need and the sufficiency of divine grace.

Dr. Charles E. Jefferson once said that if a preacher succeeds in attaining the level of eloquence three or four times in his life, he should be content. This is probably too stringent a limitation upon ministerial hope and expectancy. Indeed, when eloquence is understood as "the power to express one's self with vivid and moving force" there ought to be a degree of it in every sermon. If there should be a consistent failure at this point, it would mean that the sermon is not reaching the deeper sensibilities of the hearers, and that nothing of consequence is taking place. But the warning which this great pastor-preacher was expressing is timely in every generation. He is saying: Never strive for eloquence as if it were something to be attained within itself. Speak the truth which pertains to the needs and hungers of the present hour; speak it with all the clearness and force and fervor you can command. If the result is such that it can rightly be called eloquent, give thanks to God, not that he has made you eloquent but that the word which you have been permitted to utter has burned its way into the areas of human life where convictions are formed and decisions made. And it would be well to keep always in mind Dr. James Denney's warning that "no man can give at once the impression that he himself is clever and that Christ is mighty to save." In his own unique style, Bishop William A. Quayle wrote of this phase of the pastor's work, "When this preacher comes to a Sunday in his journey through the week, people ask him, 'Preacherman, where were you and what saw you while the workdays were sweating at their toil?' And then of this preacher we may say reverently, 'He opened his mouth and taught them, saying:' and there will be another though lesser Sermon on the Mount. And the auditors sit and sob and shout under their breath, and say with their helped hearts, 'Preacher, saw you and heard you that? You were well employed. Go out and listen and look another week; but be very sure to come back and tell us what you heard and saw.' That will be preaching." [1]

Is there any need to insist that this kind of preaching comes only at the price of unceasing toil? For a man to depend upon facility of speech and cheap plagiarisms for the substance to fill the precious twenty-five or thirty minutes which are his but once or twice a week is to trifle away his supreme opportunity to fashion the thinking and direct the decisions of his people. He is guilty of an affront against God and man. After the fullest degree of allowance is made for the unexpected outpouring of divine inspiration, there is one point upon which all effective preachers are agreed: There is no substitute for honest labor. For every five minutes of preaching Dr. Harry Emerson Fosdick spends two hours in preparation. Dr. Gerald Kennedy is convinced that "A steady habit of at least four hours a day of study is the only foundation upon which you can build an adequate preparation of sermon." The array of witnesses could be lengthened indefinitely. Dr. Frank Cairns could testify for all of them when he says, "It is my experience that there are few things God acknowledges more graciously and bountifully than hard work."

[1] *The Pastor-Preacher* (Methodist Book Concern, 1910) , p. 371.

"And ye shall teach them"

After the pastor has settled upon a plan for making the best use of the hours of public worship, he is likely to find his next ally in the teaching personnel and processes of his church. It was only a little while ago that religious education was being hailed in many quarters of Protestantism as a modern messiah that would deliver us from our antiquated methods of advancing the Kingdom and would lead us into the new day of conquest. Methods and techniques which had been discovered and tested in secular education were being introduced into the church-school, teaching was shifted from the Bible-centered to the life-centered emphasis, and there was a tendency in some parts of the country to make the director of the educational activities in large churches the executive head of the staff. The years that followed this outburst of hopeful enthusiasm brought many disillusionments. In spite of the significant and permanent contributions which resulted from the rediscovery of a neglected emphasis of the church's obligation, it must be confessed that many of the hopes which it fostered have not been fulfilled. Instead of keeping pace with the growth in population, a steady decline in enrollment and attendance was reported by the larger Protestant denominations for nearly twenty years. The difficulty of enlisting competent teachers and of securing adequate time for class sessions have been serious barriers to effective teaching. Reactionary religious groups have taken advantage of this partial failure and are presenting an interpretation of Christian truth which is out of harmony with the progress of scientific knowledge and with the spirit of the Bible itself.

It may as well be admitted that the process of maintaining a worthy system of Christian education in our American church life is exceedingly complicated. When we contrast our situation with that of a country like Sweden, where more than 90 per cent of the people are members of the Lutheran Church, and where religion is taught regularly in the public schools, we can see the extent of our confusion. With Catholics, Jews, and Protestants living together but holding to their differing concepts of what is to be taught—to say nothing of the scores of small sects, each with its own educational pattern—with the Supreme Court holding that the teaching of religion on released public-school time is unconstitutional, with the boundary between the Church and state in the realm of parochial schools not satisfactorily defined, it is not surprising that there is a vast amount of confusion as to the direction Christian education should take today. This uncertainty has resulted in a tendency on the part of some pastors to confine their activities to the minimum requirements and to disclaim all responsibility for any kind of progressive planning. But the pastor cannot escape this obligation. In spite of the disorder, there are some vitally important things that he can do now. Upon whether or not he does them will depend the direction that will be taken by lives in the making that are under his care.

By virtue of his office the pastor is the directing head of the educational system in his church. His lay helpers are not likely to place a higher appraisal upon the importance of their work than they see reflected in his attitude.

If he holds the teaching ministry of the church in slight
regard, he may count upon it that this estimate will find
expression in every department of the church's life. On
the other hand, any pastor who honestly believes in the
teaching mission of the church and is willing to work at the
job can bring an effective part of the leadership of his congregation to his point of view in three years.

It must be said, with emphasis, that no church can fulfill
its obligation to teach so long as it thinks of religious instruction as a process confined to childhood and adolescence. A congregation is really Christian only to the extent
that it is growing in its understanding of what it means
to be a follower of Christ today. This means that in most
congregations a greatly increased emphasis upon adult
education is an imperative need. In spite of all the hopeful
promise of childhood, this is an adult world. The major
decisions are made by adults. Adults are the voters. The
decisions as to what kind of religious education children
are to have and under what environment—whether in a
room comparable in light and ventilation to the public-
school classroom or in a gloomy corner of the basement—
is made by adults. What hope can there be for the in-
fusion of Christian principles into community, national,
and international life until there is a vastly larger number
of adults who are seriously seeking to know what those
principles are and how they may be put into practice today?
We may put it down, therefore, that the pastor's first obligation in the field of education is to keep before himself and his people the fact that the teaching of the Christian faith and its implications for present-day living is not

optional but stands at the very center of the church's mission.

A second point at which the pastor faces a responsibility is in the training of teachers. He may either do this himself through periodic training classes or he may find in the congregation more capable leadership than he could offer. Some small churches are fortunate in being related to a group ministry where one of the pastors give special attention to this phase of parish life. Many churches in which there is the feeling that a director of Christian education would be an intolerable financial burden are amply able to employ such a person, at least on a part-time basis. Although there are 120,000 American children who attend Protestant parochial schools, it is not likely that Christian education in the Protestant Church will move in that direction. We cannot withhold commendation from the church whose members are so much concerned about the religious instruction of their children that they are willing to bear the additional expense of maintaining schools where religion is a part of the curriculum. The public school is an American institution and a logical ally of the home and the Church in the formation of character. But it cannot do the work of all three. Until the Protestant Church takes more seriously its obligation to give religious instruction to its children and youth, with the consequent expense of money and energy, it cannot hope to release the powers that are latent in its message.

The educational processes of the local church are not confined to the classroom and the pulpit. They include every activity of the church which results in the changing or developing of attitudes. An example of this is the pastor's

68

never-ending obligation to keep his congregation aware of its missionary responsibilty. The missionary spirit is inherent in the Christian religion, but its operation in the life of the individual church member or of a congregation cannot be taken for granted. The pull of isolationism in the realm of religion is strong and constant. Lack of knowledge, preoccupation, indifference, and complacency all unite to direct the attention of a church away from its world connections. And then there is a short-sighted view —preachers are not immune to it—that whatever a congregation gives to missions reduces, by so much, the available support for work within the parish. The truth is that the local church rarely suffers financially from insufficiency of resources. Its real problem is lack of liberality. Where the attention of a congregation is constantly directed to its own local needs, the roots of selfishness choke the springs of generosity not only for missions but ultimately for its own needs. This process at work in the churches registers itself in a penurious level of per capita giving for missions and in an insufficient number of young people who are offering themselves for missionary service. There is no more certain way to develop and maintain a spirit of generosity which blesses everything it touches than by keeping a congregation awake to its essential world outreach.

Beyond all this, it is impossible to maintain the spirit of true Christianity in a congregation that is not aware of its relation to a world movement. Numerous agencies, including the press, the radio, and motion pictures, are directing the thought of the people to internationalism in political, economic, and military terms. Almost single handed the Church faces the responsibility of emphasizing the fact that already a uniting faith—the Christian religion—is manifesting itself as an international force that must be reckoned with. Men who are acquainted with the world scene tell us that Christianity is more deeply rooted among more peoples than it or any other religion or any body of ideas has ever been before. The missionary movement in the modern phase is little more than a century and a half old. Serious effort at international cooperation began less than fifty years ago. We must confess that the movement has not yet been able to command the devotion of more than a minority of church members, and the level of giving in money and personnel indicates that it is still a marginal interest in American Protestantism. And yet the power which it has exerted in releasing streams of civilizing forces and in influencing world affairs is out of all proportion to the personnel and material resources involved. Even in the face of an aggressive communism and a crippling secularism, no man can fix the limits to what an awakened and committed Church could do even in this generation to change the moral and spiritual climate of the world. The pastor who recognizes early in his ministry that in a real sense he stands by the side of his college or seminary mate who serves in another land will find his own life deepened and enlarged and will be able to keep his congregation aware of a fellowship that is wide enough for the Spirit of Christ.

Visiting and counseling

The third major method of ministering to the lives of people—and of changing them—is through pastoral visiting and counseling. In spite of all the labor-saving devices of modern life no substitute has been found, or can ever be found, for pastoral calling. Methods of rapid and multiple communication have greatly enlarged the area of the pastoral touch but there is an irreducible minimum of human need which can be met in no way except by the process of personal contact. A vast amount of scorn has been released upon the alleged waste of time that is spent in ringing doorbells when there are so many more important things to be done. All of this is a cheap effort to justify laziness or indifference and is not worthy either of the tradition of the Protestant ministry or of the possibility for good which intelligent, unceasing, pastoral calling holds today. It is not easy work. That is the chief reason why we are constantly tempted to turn away from it and to seek excuses for not doing it. No man can make himself available to the variety and depth of human need which a pastor meets in a typical afternoon of visitation without feeling the drain of spiritual energies. Many times I have recalled the statement of a seminary teacher who had been a pastor himself: "I never went out to an afternoon of pastoral calling without compelling myself to go; I never came back without the feeling that I had been in at least one home at a providential hour." The latter part of the experience recurs so frequently that the pastor is brought to the conviction that in the choice of homes in which he will call there is an element of guidance by the Shepherd of all souls. In going for him and with him there is compensation for the struggle with the flesh which is required.

What proportion of his time should the minister spend in pastoral calling? Few questions concerning the pastoral office would call out a wider range of answers than this one. For nearly ten years I have had access to the quarterly records of more than nine hundred pastors who report the number of calls made. The totals vary widely. This is due, in part, to differences in distances involved and in the definition of what constitutes a pastoral call. But the more significant reason for the variation is the measure of importance which different men assign to the obligation of the pastoral ministry. My own conviction is that five afternoons each week should be spent in purposeful calling and that, unless the homes of the parish are widely separated, twelve hundred calls a year should be regarded as a minimum number.

The pastor who demonstrates to his people his own belief in the worth of this phase of his ministry will usually have no great difficulty in enlisting his members in fulfilling their share of this activity. Without this sustained interest no parish can be held together as a living organism. Various modifications of the "unit system" are being used to locate responsibility and to provide lay oversight for each home in the parish. At least twice each year there should be a complete and unhurried church-wide visitation—one to secure pledges to the annual budget and the other to publicize such special activities as the period of evangelism or family week. The by-products of this visitation in terms of individual fellowship and current information will be almost as valuable as achieving the main objective. This kind of lay participation does not come spontaneously, but it can be secured if pastors care enough.

The newest and in many respects the most alluring method of helping people with moral and spiritual difficulties is pastoral counseling. Its basic techniques are as old as the Christian religion but the effort to apply the findings of modern psychology to the problems of pastoral guidance has resulted in this new approach. It brings with it both exciting possibilities and subtle dangers. One of the disillusioning experiences which come to the young pastor in this field is the undramatic quality of most of the problems which people bring for solution. He recalls the classroom discussion in the seminary and the typical "cases" which he read in the books on pastoral psychiatry and expects that the sin-ridden will promptly come to him with their confessions of guilt and their hungers for spiritual guidance. Instead of this it is far more likely that those who do venture in to see him will want to talk with him about financial worries, unemployment, domestic disharmony and and a score of more or less minor ills. Indeed, one of the pastor's problems in this phase of his ministry is to discriminate between those who have urgent needs which he can help to relieve and those who find a morbid delight in confessing or who have nothing more entertaining for the hour than to visit with the pastor. It must always be remembered that many persons whose need is most critical will not go to the pastor for help. He must go to them. Directed by a sensitiveness to human need, he must find them and skillfully open the way for the revealing of their burdens.

Without attempting to give detailed directions for pastoral counseling—these can be found in many good books by specialists in the field—the following elementary but basically important suggestions are made. First, begin each interview that involves a problem with the conviction that there is a Christian way out of every situation. It may not be easy to find that way nor to follow it when it is found. But there are no hopeless cases, and the shortest step in the right direction makes the next one easier. Second, develop the art of sympathetic listening. This is not done without effort by men who are accustomed to attach great importance to their own gifts of speech. But it is imperative if the way is to be kept open for the word that can guide and heal. The fact is, many a problem is half solved when the person who is troubled by it brings it into the open with a frank statement. The gift for asking the right questions is often as important as knowing the correct answer. Third, never appear unduly surprised or shocked; do not become argumentative; do not condemn. Few if any cases will be met in which the requirements of Christian behavior are not already quite clearly known. Fourth, use every means to bring the distressed person to a reliance upon God rather than upon the sympathy or wisdom of the counselor. Direction in the forming of habits of private devotions is greatly needed by most people. The proper use of such devotional material as Bishop Ralph S. Cushman's *Pocket Prayer Book* and Dr. Bonnell's *How to Read the Bible* can be made a hopeful beginning. Fifth, hold everything that is revealed in the course of such a conversation as a sacred trust. The most effectual method that could be devised for closing the door through which the needy and disturbed might come to the pastor for help would be for him to disclose, in conversation or public address, even under cover of altered names, any experience that has been entrusted to him in the confidence of a pastoral interview.

74

In his effort to help his people in the realm of personality problems the pastor is sometimes tempted to employ the techniques of psychiatry even when he has no background of knowledge or training to warrant the attempt. This fascination is probably traceable to two sources: first, the alluring mysteries of the human mind with its amazing capacity for unaccountable behavior and, second, the belief, now largely discounted, that the use of the proper psychological procedure will result in transformations comparable to sudden conversion which can make unnecessary the slower processes of nurture and training.

All temptations in the direction of amateur psychiatry are to be firmly resisted. The processes of the human mind, even in a disordered condition, are too delicately balanced to be trifled with by one who attempts to use methods of analysis and cure with which he is only slightly acquainted. There are areas of ministry to men and women who are bedeviled by fear and inward defeat which belong to the pastor on the warrant of the New Testament and Christian experience. It is doubtful whether the theories of modern psychology have advanced, with soundness, beyond the description of the age-old conflict described in the seventh and eight chapters of Romans. Notable progress has been made toward an understanding between pastors and psychiatrists as to ways in which they can work together in restoring the mentally disturbed to sanity and health. But there are many psychiatrists who have not yet escaped from the anti-religious bias of Freud and his disciples. The most dependable barrier against the tide of nervous and mental affliction which threatens the American people could be discerning pastors who know how to make available to

75

confused and baffled souls the resources of the Christian faith.

Dr. John Mathews, an unusually effective pastor of an earlier generation, wrote in his autobiography, "For more than forty years I have studied the easy passes into the human heart." I wonder if this is not, after all, the pastor's main business. This may seem, at first, to be too restricted an endeavor for strong men in a day when world forces of tremendous power are on the march. And yet all of these forces are controlled by individual men. There is no hope that they will ever be directed into more constructive channels until men's hearts are changed. The dictator seeks the same approach to the inner courts of the human soul. But he goes in to bind and enslave. The pastor enters to heal and to set free. These two represent opposing forces that, through the centuries, have been contending with each other but never with quite so much intensity as today. The future of mankind depends upon which of the two can, in greater numbers, find and travel "the easy passes to the human heart."

IV

MY FELLOW WORKER

THERE IS NO PART OF A PASTOR'S MINISTRY THAT CAN BRING to him more joy and satisfaction, if properly managed, or more irritation and grief, if improperly handled, than his relation to the laymen of his church. If the preacher were thinking in no higher terms than his own enjoyment of his vocation, it would be important for him to give careful consideration to this relationship which begins the first day he enters a parish, and before, and continues to the last day, and after. But when he thinks in terms of the growth of the Kingdom of God he is compelled to make decision as to what place the layman must assume. Some men enter the ministry with a distorted conception of the layman's place in the church and of the pastor's relation to him. They think of him as one who is basically unfriendly to the church and whose connection with it is a matter of discharging a duty or of pleasing his wife. They meet a sufficient number of laymen of this type to confirm their suspicions, and some of them go on for years before they discover how much stimulating and enlightening comradeship they have been missing. Other preachers have a false conception of the layman's ability to comprehend spiritual things. He may do well enough, they think, in attending to the temporal affairs of the church, but in matters that require spiritual discernment the layman cannot qualify. This fallacious notion is the basis of all ministerial dictatorship.

And then there are young pastors who have had only limited opportunity to become acquainted with men in the normal setting of their weekday toil, particularly with men who have no connection with the church. A chaplain who had just returned from the service said, "My duties brought me into contact with men of all kinds of religious background—and none. From now on I think I know how to approach any man and talk with him about Christianity, beginning where he is." I have had the opportunity to observe some of the positive results of this pastor's wider contact with men. Before this experience he had scarcely been beyond the orbit of the Church's life. He was born in a parsonage, grew up in a preacher's home, went away to a church college and then to a theological seminary and from there to another parsonage. What opportunity had he found to get a firsthand acquaintance with men who lived outside the inner circle of the church? It scarcely needs to be said that the chaplaincy is not the only means of enlarging this area of experience.

"This man eats with sinners"

There is no evidence that Jesus was ever hindered in his ministry by a barrier between himself and the men of his day. This freedom from restraint was one of the results of the years he spent in a carpenter shop and in all the relationships that went with thirty years of small-town life. He believed in men—even in their hidden possibilities— and his confidence in them caused them to leave their nets and their tax books and go with him. The bond of comradeship which was begun with the first acquaintance grew stronger as they came to know him better. This friendship was not simply one in which he gave to them and they received from him. They provided for him a fellowship which he needed and desired. They often failed him, but the fact that his longing for them in the hour of his agony was so real is evidence that he felt a sense of dependence upon them. Were these men ministers or laymen? I once heard a group of preachers debate the question—inconclusively. I do not know the answer, nor do I think it greatly matters.

Jesus did not limit his association to the people who were in good standing with the church of his day. One of the frequent charges which his enemies brought against him was that he ate with publicans and sinners. And he did not go to their homes to condemn. Men do not willingly invite a dinner guest because they want to be told of their sins. They invited Jesus to their tables because they liked him. There is probably no ministerial gift that is in greater need of cultivation than that of getting beyond the barrier to men who have never had a fair chance to see what genuine Christianity is like.

This attitude of understanding and appreciation was a notable quality in the life of Paul. It is altogether likely that this virtue, like all of his best attributes, came to him as the result of his fellowship with Christ. His arrogant spirit and his rabbinical training combined to make him contemptuous of individual worth. But from the moment a man named Ananias came to him in his blindness, laid his hands upon him, and called him "Brother Saul" to his last day in a Roman prison from which he wrote a letter about a runaway slave to a layman whom he knew, his devotion to his fellow Christians continued to grow. He discovered that in Christ the old barriers that had isolated men into a priestly caste had been removed. He found the blessings of fellowship with men and women who were telling others of this new way of life by the authority of an ordination that transcends ecclesiastical sanctions. His letters are interspersed with greetings and personal messages to those who had befriended him, had worked with him, and had shared with him the stigma and the joy of being followers of the Galilean. At the end of his letter to the Christians in Rome he mentions by name twenty-seven persons and several families to whom he sends messages of affection—a few names kept from oblivion of the hundreds he must have counted as his friends and fellow-workers. Jesus and Paul gave to Christian preachers an example of fellowship with laymen which sets the standard and reveals the method.

The priesthood of all believers

There is no area of our Protestant church life that is in greater need just now of capable research and frank discussion than is the Christian conception of the place of the layman in the Church. In the Roman Catholic Church the line of demarcation between the priesthood and the laity is clearly drawn and its implications are understood by those who stand on either side. In the Protestant Church we run the full gamut from the point where all believers are held to be ministers to the high-church usage, which comes close to excluding the layman from everything except the outer courts of the temple. I am not assuming that such a study as is suggested would result in uniformity of practice, but it would enable us to understand more clearly where the basic norm is to be found.

Such an inquiry as this is likely to reveal the fact that some of the erroneous notions from which Protestantism rebelled have been perpetuated in her own blood stream. Upon one principle I think there would be almost unanimous agreement: The New Testament conception of the priesthood is not that one man is set apart, by ecclesiastical ceremonial, to perform on behalf of other men certain sacred rites connected with worship and absolution from sin. It is rather that one man, by virtue of special fitness and training, is commissioned to open the way and to lead the entire worshiping congregation into the very presence of God. The "priesthood of all believers" is not a concept born with the Reformation but is a relationship between God and man which is implicit in the whole Christian revelation. It is made specific in giving to Christ, who is the embodiment of the eternal priesthood, the designation of the "Pioneer of our salvation."

One of the reasons for hesitancy on the part of some ministers in encouraging lay participation is the fear that the laymen, with their lack of understanding of the mission of the Church, will retard its progress. There is no basis for this fear. Without regard to possibilities in a church that is governed by a priestly hierarchy, it is a settled fact that Protestantism can never move forward more rapidly than it is able to carry with it the rank and file of its laity. Principal Macgregor of Scotland was once warning young preachers against the danger of rushing into the main points of a sermon before the congregation had been given the opportunity to see which way the preacher proposed to lead them. He said, "We all, on occasion, must have seen a preacher starting off in a blaze of passion before his people were well settled in their pews, and it has looked like nothing in the world but a railway engine snorting away before it has been coupled to its train. There was noise and energy enough for anything, but the passengers stayed where they were." This principle is applicable to the relation which a pastor has to the laymen of his church. It is of no great consequence how fast or how far he travels unless he is able to carry with him at least a substantial element of his congregation. In the New Testament conception of the term, preaching is more than an individual performance—it is the corporate witness of the group. Preaching that is really forceful is the setting forth of moral and spiritual truth which is being exemplified in the lives of the church members. If the people move slowly and reluctantly, it will require from the preacher the patience to wait until the forces of education and persuasion have been given the chance to change the atmosphere. Rash ultimatums are rarely in order. It is a sad day in the life of the Church—local or general—when a cleavage develops between the ministry and the laity which makes it difficult to recognize the common interests and goals which bind them together.

It is a fallacy to assume that the initiative for moral and spiritual progress is limited to the ministry. The history of the Hebrew-Christian religion gives repeated denial to any such idea. Abraham, Moses, David, and the greatest of the eighth century prophets were laymen. Religious movements in the Middle Ages, within the Catholic

Church and on the outside, were largely motivated and directed by laymen. The modern missionary movement was born in the heart of laymen. In giving thanks for the Student Volunteer Movement and the World's Student Christian Federation, it must be remembered that Dr. John R. Mott is a layman. It is impossible to measure the influence which laymen whose names have not been conspicuous have exerted in giving the propulsion of loyalty and devotion to evangelistic and reform movements within the Church. Nor can enough gratitude be expressed for the service they have rendered to the Protestant Church in helping to guard it against the dangers of priestcraft and professionalism.

Effective planning for the Church requires an intelligent understanding of the issues involved and the giving of the necessary time for attendance at assemblies. The meeting of these conditions requires more than ordinary concern for the welfare of the Church. But they are requirements that cannot be evaded and the Church will move forward haltingly until a larger proportion of laymen are willing to fulfill them. It is said—and I think correctly— that laymen are impatient at the slowness with which plans for church union are advancing. They want the churches which are ready for the step to unite now. But are these laymen willing to spend the time and effort that are required for formulating plans of union that will result in unity rather than confusion and dissension? How is the layman to be informed about the history of his church, its form of government, its plans of advance unless he reads its literature and attends its conferences and conventions? How can he reach an intelligent view of the place which the missionary enterprise must have in building a dependable world unless he is willing to examine the essential facts? This knowledge comes through the same process by which he learns about the things that are related to his business or profession. An invitation to participate is not enough; there must be a positive response. The Church must not be unrealistic in its requirements upon the layman's weekday time, but the large attendance at fraternal, civic and political conventions is an indication that far more time can be found than is now being used. The training and development of a larger body of lay churchmen who can take their places, constructively, in the assemblies of the Church is a joint responsibility of the clergy and laity.

Get acquainted with your laymen

To go beyond the conventional limits of the pastor-layman relationship will require time and, in some cases, the grace of patience. Many laymen have had very limited opportunity to become closely acquainted with a preacher. Even though they have belonged to the Church for many years their contacts with their pastors have been largely at the professional level. They have thought of preachers as belonging to a distinct order of mankind. These men need to be given the opportunity to know their pastor as a human being. The furthering of this kind of fellowship will bring big rewards. The young pastor will soon discover that Gerald Kennedy is correct in saying that "For every mean, narrow-minded, bickering layman with a Nero-complex, there are a dozen devoted, loyal, generous churchmen." And it must be remembered that the most contentious layman in the congregation has somewhere stood at the altar of the church to assume the vows of faithfulness to Christ and of service to his fellow man. This means that at one time he was impelled by an unselfish motive and that he is not beyond hope.

Get acquainted with all your laymen. You will soon discover that they differ widely in their ways of responding to the call of Christ through the Church. Some belong to the introspective, meditative type with a touch of the mystical which makes the devotional life of the Christian faith a congenial exercise. This would probably be a larger group if the pattern of our secular life were not so largely set in the direction of strenuous exertion. Other men respond almost wholly in terms of outward activity. They are not greatly impressed by ritual and ceremony but they are easy to enlist in enterprises where results are tangible and visible. These two types of men need each other and their fellowship should be encouraged. The impact of the Church upon the world about it can never be all that it should be until both of these groups find the fullest expression of their special endowments.

Pastors are sometimes guilty of neglecting the obscure and socially unpretentious members of their congregations. This is a type of unfaithfulness which cannot be condoned. No part of the pastor's commission is so frequently reiterated in the New Testament as his charge to care for the poor. But it is an offense equally grave and probably more frequently committed to neglect the man who is prominent and materially successful. It is easy to take for granted that his self-sufficiency is such that he is not aware of any need which the Church can supply. This is a false

85

assumption. Behind many a façade of worldy success there is an emptiness of heart which does not readily reveal itself. Men who might have been strong personal forces in advancing the Kingdom have missed the joy of it because their pastors thought they were too busy to be disturbed by requests for anything beyond financial support. In the fellowship of Christ's people men stand before God on one level, without respect to social prominence or material possessions. The urgency of men's need constitutes the only priority of demand upon a pastor's time.

Let no preacher suppose that the benefits of his association with laymen, in terms of spiritual enrichment, will be one-way traffic. A discerning pastor will approach this fellowship in a mood to receive as well as to give. If I were called upon to say from which group, ministers or laymen, I have received more help in my own efforts at religious living, it would not be easy to say. Many a pastor has found his own faith renewed and the breadth of his thinking about the activities of his church enlarged through fellowship with devoted and understanding laymen. It is only through such association that the pastor becomes familiar with some of the problems that disturb and complicate the lives of laymen in their attempts to maintain the Christian standard in an unfriendly world. Fortunate is the preacher who has the unreserved confidence of a group of laymen through whose eyes he is permitted to see the Church and its mission. If he does not make use of the resources—material and spiritual—which they control he is robbing himself and his church of available forces that can change weakness into strength.

Within the body of the total membership there should

be the inner circle of men who are capable of bearing special responsibility. When Jesus spent two or three years in intimate association with twelve men as a means of imparting to them an understanding of the new Kingdom and of the methods of its growth, he gave an example of how the Church is to be extended. This plan has never been displaced by a better one. Some pastors will seek to dismiss the suggestion with the reply that there are not twelve men in their parishes who have enough spiritual perception to become members of such an inner fellowship. These men should read again the record of patient endeavor which Jesus put into the training of the Twelve and of the repeated disappointment he suffered from their slowness to learn and their contentious bickering which continued even to the Upper Room. But, with one exception, they could not escape the meaning of his revelation and in the power of the larger faith they stood firm in their final hour of testing. You will sometimes be fortunate enough to find such a group of men ready at hand in the new parish; in other instances you will be compelled to start almost from the beginning. But the men are there, either in the Church or out of it, and finding them and bringing their unused talents into the service of the Kingdom is a thrilling experience.

The grace of liberality

This is probably the best place for a word about an area of the pastor's relationship with his laymen which can be either a burden or a blessing: his obligation to help them in arriving at a Christian standard of stewardship. Most pastors at the beginning of their ministry long for a congregation in which the entire responsibility for planning and administering the financial system can be committed to the laymen. They feel that for them to encumber themselves with so mundane a part of the life of the church is an encroachment upon the more spiritual elements of their vocation. They either attempt to wash their hands of the whole thing or they attend to it with reluctance and a sense of inner resentment. In most instances when a pastor shirks his duty at this point, the result is a loose and ineffective plan of church finance—one which does not command available financial resources and leads to a deficit in the monthly financial statement. More serious than either of these is the inexcusable failure to give to members of the church the kind of training that is required for intelligent and joyful participation in the financial life of the church. The pastor's direct appeal to a layman for financial support for a worthy cause frequently opens the way to a discussion that results in a changed attitude toward stewardship and a revised method of giving.

Even in the few unusual cases where there are lay officials who are able to give successful direction to this phase of church activity, the understanding counsel of the pastor is still required. The financing of a church is not simply a matter of getting enough money to pay the bills. It is a means of cultivating a Christian attitude toward material wealth and an intelligent understanding of the financial requirements of the church. For this reason it should never be separated from the larger aspects of the Christian gospel. For a pastor to say, "I do not care to know how much any member or family in my congregation contributes to the church" is equivalent to saying, "I am not interested in knowing to what extent my people are growing in the grace of Christian generosity." Instead of shrinking from this obligation as a distasteful chore he should welcome it as the opportunity for developing in the lives of his members a basic Christian virtue.

The church member's acceptance of the principle of Christian stewardship with respect to material possessions solves a multitude of problems for himself and for his church. Like other Christian virtues, the grace of liberality cannot be developed in a vacuum. The hours the pastor spends with the finance committee in arriving at a sound budget, in preparing for the every-member canvass and arranging for special financial appeals are not to be written off as a reluctant concession to an unwelcome requirement. They are to be recognized as his distinctive opportunity to add a new dimension to the lives of people. If he was not taught in seminary the principles of sound church finance, he had better lose no time after he gets out in learning them from the best books on the subject and from the wisest counselors. It is an obligation which will always be with him whether he ministers in small churches or large ones. It is the pastor's privilege to make a sacrament of necessity and to find a joyful sense of satisfaction in what would otherwise have been an irksome requirement.

God and the day's work

In the Christian idea of the sacredness of every vocation that serves human need lies the only effective method of combatting the corrosive spirit of secularism which is the greatest single threat to the Christian way of life. One of the pernicious results of drawing a distinct line of demarcation between the ministry and the laity is the tendency to regard one group as engaged in serving the Lord while the other follows selfish aims with only so much homage to religion as is necessary to insure success and a reasonably untroubled conscience. Nothing could be more foreign to the spirit and temper of the New Testament. Use all available means to make your laymen understand this.

Every man's craft or calling should be to him the daily opportunity for service to man and God. He does not need to go beyond it to find fellowship with his Father who is also at work. He welcomes the opportunities of worship not because his relation to God is limited to these special seasons but because through these high moments there shines a light that illumines the whole range of his experience. This is the Christian conception of vocation. In this day of materialistic standards and of secular ideals, it is in grave danger of being lost. Only the Church can rescue and redeem it.

I recall in one of my own parishes a surgeon who is a specialist in correcting bone deformities of children. I have watched his skillful touch as he was adjusting these defects and giving to a child the opportunity to approach life without a physical handicap. It was a privilege to help this physician of the body to interpret his mission as a part of the will and purpose of the healing Christ. In another church there was a chemical engineer who had developed a special process for refining gasoline. As we stood together one night on a runway overlooking his section of the refinery he said, "This is my job. I feel that I am serving God through it as truly as when I do the things which we usually think of as religious duties." Who among us has not known teachers who, in spite of small pay and meager expressions of appreciation, have gone on year after year refusing to be lured away by larger incomes and imparting to successive generations of youth something that cannot be put into books. The list might be lengthened almost indefinitely.

It must be acknowledged that there are kinds of toil which have so little of intrinsic appeal to the creative instincts as to be unrelieved drudgery. How can it be expected that a man will regard such employment as being anything other than a kind of slavery from which he has found no way of escape? What place is there for the idea of divine vocation? Two things need to be said. First, no matter how much of distasteful labor there is about an uninspiring job, if it is essential to human welfare it is possible for a man with a Christian outlook to develop toward it an attitude of pride in doing it with maximum efficiency. Second, the hours of labor and the scale of pay for this kind of toil should be such that men who are engaged in it shall have sufficient time each day for activities that are congenial and rewarding.

Holding the world together

A third suggestion to the pastor concerning his relationship to his laymen is that he help them to understand that they are engaged in creating and maintaining a brotherhood. That is New Testament language but there have been times when it appeared to be in more frequent use outside the Church than on the inside.

Out of all the turmoil and confusion of the present world

situation there emerges one crucial question: How can all of us manage to live together in some degree of harmony on this small planet? With the continued increase of population and the elemental drives of overcongested peoples for a fairer share of the earth's resources this question becomes more urgent every year. Many answers are offered but upon examination they all prove to be variations of two major plans. According to one of these proposals the world can be held together if one nation or group of nations amasses so much destructive power that the rest of the world will be kept in subjection by cringing fear. This is the method of tyranny and imperialism. It is as old as man's first efforts toward civilization. It has been attempted again and again but has never succeeded for any considerable period of time. The reason for its failure is that when God created man he put into his heart an instinctive love for freedom which, sooner or later, asserts itself with sufficient fury to break its chains. Dictatorship is not a workable plan.

The second method of securing world order is based upon the convictions that no race or nation has the right to oppress another, that every individual has an inherent right to a decent chance at life, that there can be no security anywhere until there is security everywhere, and that the only kind of world order that can endure will be built, not upon force and fear, but upon justice and intelligent good will. The peril of a statement like this—which almost everybody accepts as being true—is the assumption that to put these precepts into operation we must begin at the international level. As a matter of fact we can never begin at that level. The only effective place to begin is within a group that is small enough for the principles of acquaintance and appreciation and brotherly co-operation to be a realized ideal. A nation's most dependable bulwark against any form of dictatorship is found in a sufficient number of small groups of men and women who are committed to the conviction that if confronted by the demand to put the state above the laws of God, they must obey God rather than men. This is the vitally important sector which the Church holds in the life of America and of the world. From this base line we are ready to move out into a wider orbit with the realization that there are some things in this world that can be done only by numbers.

The conscience of the state

The Church has written a widely varied record in its relation to the state and to what we call the secular order. During the Middle Ages the Church dominated the state and, to a very high degree, was a unifying force in the realm of thought and morals. In conformity with the principle that "power corrupts" the Church of that period became lax and worldly to such an extent that the Reformation become inevitable. In recent times there have been notable examples of attempts by the Church to detach itself from all responsibility for governmental affairs. It has said to the agents of the state, "So long as you do not encroach upon the domain of our individual, mystical, relation to God we have no concern for the manner in which you conduct affairs that are purely political." The disastrous results in more than one nation of that kind of desertion of the Church's mission can never be forgotten. In the light of this history it should be plain to us that while the

Church is not to control the state after the medieval pattern, it must be the conscience of the political and economic order and must assert its authority at whatever cost to speak for God even when its voice is in direct variance from current policies. This mission can be effectively discharged only through the life and influence of informed and devoted laymen.

When laymen are responsive to their obligation to the Church, they can keep it flexible and reasonably free from the blight of ecclesiastical narrowness. One of the perils of the Church is the tendency to become self-conscious and more concerned about its own welfare than about its mission. The priest is predominantly on the defensive. There is a constant pull toward exclusiveness and a deadening regularity of procedure. It is exceedingly hard to keep the Church from defining life in terms that are too narrow to make room for this greatness of God. Perhaps this is what Archbishop Temple had in mind when he said, "It is a great mistake to suppose that God is only, or even chiefly, concerned with religion." Many an ecclesiastical blunder could have been avoided if the point of view of the intelligent layman had been taken into account.

Christianity will never get to the heart of the disturbed areas of race relations, industrial conflict, and political activity until laymen take it there. The Church of England has recently announced, "We are convinced that England will never be converted until the laity use the opportunities for evangelism daily afforded by their various professions, crafts and occupations. . . . The Christian laity should be recognized as the true priesthood of the Church in the working world, and as the Church militant in action in the mission field of politics, industry and commerce." In recalling laymen with whom he had worked, Dr. Fosdick says, "They carried Christ where I could never go; they exhibited the Christian spirit in relationships I never had a chance at; they wrought reforms in their businesses and professions that were utterly beyond my reach; they served the community in ways that no minister can compass, and put their intelligence and skill at the disposal of the Church, with results that I never dreamed were possible. Don't tell me that men and women are not called of God to Christian laymanship." [2]

A second look at the layman

What do you see, brother pastor, in that layman who sits before you on Sunday morning? A man who came to church because it is a family custom, and who will feel a sense of relief when he hears the benediction? A man so engrossed in the struggles of a competitive society that the things which you are soon to say about faith and brotherliness will have a far-off sound to him as if they did not belong to the world he lives in? A man so much a part of his day that all the fears and lusts and anxieties and hopes of his race are so mixed up in him that the only thing he is sure of is that he wants safety and a fair degree of plenty for himself and his family? If that is all you see, then you see only a part of the man who is there. This man belongs to a race that has produced adventurers and explorers and pioneers who have crossed uncharted oceans in little ships that were scarcely seaworthy, who have dared all the perils of the wilderness and the mountains and the deserts—men

[2] *Laymen Speaking* (Association Press, 1947), p. 19.

who have taken their lives in their hands and have gone out not knowing whither they went. This man is closely related to men who have pledged their property, their lives, and their sacred honor in defense of causes they believed were just. He probably does not know it, as he sits there fumbling the church bulletin and wondering about income tax and elections and the trend of the wheat market, but in his heart are smoldering fires that could be stirred to such a flame that he would do valiant things for God and man which he does not now dream he could ever do. He thinks he is religiously unemotional, but men like him have bowed, rank upon rank, before the winds of God like fields of grain. He is not far removed from men who have gone into temples and have seen the Lord and felt the refining fires of forgiveness; and when they heard a voice saying, "Whom shall I send?" they replied, without regard to the darkness and danger of the continent of need, "Here am I, send me." More than once, at the call of a crusading leader, they have left their farms and families and have gone in the face of hardship and death into a strange land to rescue a holy shrine. You would hardly believe it, knowing how little this man has done to witness for his faith, but he is in line of succession to men who have gone to prison and even to death rather than renounce their allegiance to Christ. This is not fiction but sober history. And the record is not limited to a few select individuals of royal birth, but it is written of whole companies who believed themselves to be only ordinary men. What has been may be again.

Look once more, brother pastor, for this is exactly the man who sits before you. He is not so stolid and predictable as you thought him to be. It may be that some word which God allows you to speak, even today, will set the bells to ringing in this man's soul and another miracle of grace will be wrought. It could be that he will see Christ today and like another man in a far-off town called Jericho he will invite him into his heart and home in a way that he has never done before. Could there be anything more wonderful than the chance to deal with such a reality in such a day!

V

THAT THEY MAY ALL BE ONE

THE PASTOR OF THIS GENERATION WILL BE COMPELLED TO reckon with the ecumenical movement—one of the most creative currents that flows through Christendom today. Jesus prayed for his followers "that they may all be one." Not since this prayer was first uttered has there been such urgent necessity for its fulfillment as there is today. The unity of Christians is more than a devout aspiration; it is essential if the Church is to be a world community of faith which transcends the barriers of nationality, race, and class. The pastor's basic attitude toward this movement will be a large factor in determining the range and depth of his ministry.

I have no thought of discussing either the history of church mergers and federations or the procedure by which such agreements are reached in denominational councils. Our concern here is with the relation of these movements to the local congregation and to the individual Christian. In the effort to achieve church union it has repeatedly been found that the chief hindrance is not the failure of denominational leaders to reach an agreement but the unwillingness of church members to approve the proposed plan of union. The two elements of the church's organizational life, the representative assembly and the local congregation, must move forward together. Here we are dealing with inter-church co-operation at the point where the pastor is frequently the decisive factor.

The incessant pull toward unity

A primary fact to be considered is that the idea of an ecumenical church will be an increasingly influential one during the period immediately before us. The thirty-eight years which intervened between the World Missionary Conference at Edinburgh in 1910 and the first plenary session of the World Council of Churches in Amsterdam in 1948 have witnessed, in spite of two world wars, a growing sense of unity in the non-Roman section of Christendom that had scarcely been dreamed of at the beginning of this century. In his book *Toward a United Church*— which every pastor should read unless he has found the same facts in another form—Dr. William Adams Brown says, "The possibility that with the Ecumenical Movement a new chapter in Christian history has begun must not be ruled out."

The pastor who does not keep informed concerning this movement will rob himself and his people of the strength which comes from active participation in a world Church. A divided Church finds itself embarrassed and reduced in effectiveness when it attempts to speak to the nations about the necessity for co-operation. No organization in the interest of world order can hope to succeed simply as a body. It must have a soul. Such a soul can be adequately supplied only by a world Church which is united in its basic faith and its supreme purpose. The experience of more than ten million young Americans in the second world war is a factor in the religious life of the nation which cannot be ignored. Returning chaplains have emphasized, again and again, the lack of interest of Protestant servicemen in denominational differences.

Chaplain Winston L. King makes this statement of his observations: "In the daily grind of military life denominationalism was almost indistinguishable, and in crises it did not seem to matter. To be sure, there was no positive, vital sense of the Christian character of advance toward church co-operation or unity, only a blank stare of incomprehension concerning the whole matter. But the net result, positive, negative, or neutral, is the same: the heyday of denominationalism is long since past. And the urgency for realizing this is the greater precisely because of the widespread indifference to denomination, for with many it is either a co-operating and more united Protestantism or nothing at all—and that quite soon." [1]

Another fact to be taken into account is that this will not, in all places, be a popular movement. It encounters all of the obstacles to change which grow up around long-established patterns of opinion and practice. It involves the surrender of certain ideas of ecclesiastical superiority which are very precious. It calls for the abrogation of indefensible claims of denominational sovereignty. It cuts through the lines of fixed prejudices and compels us to look at ourselves through the eyes of others. It sometimes requires the slowing down of denominational machinery in the interest of the wider fellowship. And yet in spite of all these difficulties, this movement is commanding the loyalty of an increasing number of young ministers. They

1 *Christendom,* autumn, 1946.

recognize in it the only channel through which the full power of the Church can be released.

A third observation is that this movement will not be a rapid one. Patience and persistence will be required of those who work at it. This is not surprising when we consider that we are here dealing with an area of human life where dependable change is slow. Men and women who take their church membership seriously do not lightly abandon the idea that there is something distinctive about the church of their fathers and of their childhood memories. This is the element in human steadfastness that has kept men true to their faith in the fires of persecution. It is of such priceless value that the only justification for attempting to unsettle it is that it may be enlarged and centered in a higher loyalty. With all of the slowness which this process involves it must be remembered that in certain instances after long years of discouraging failure to make noticeable progress, changes of attitude have quickly matured of such consequence that a long step forward could be taken. We should take courage from such examples as the United Church of Canada, which has been moving steadily forward in spite of obstructions since its organization twenty-three years ago and the recent organization of the Church of South India, which brings into organic union five communions with a combined membership of a quarter of a million. But, slowly or rapidly, the call of this day is that we move forward.

Church or sect

What can a pastor do now as his part in lessening the breaches that divide the Body of Christ? First, by preaching, teaching, and the administering of the sacraments, he can keep his congregation aware of the essential unity of the Church. The differences which separate us are relatively minor; the basically important elements of our faith are held by all Christians. It is not so much a matter of creating a spirit of unity as of recognizing and emphasizing that which already exists. In the reception of members and in the sacraments of baptism and Holy Communion there is the recurring opportunity to give dramatic emphasis to this New Testament conception of the oneness of the followers of Christ. We must never forget that in the last analysis the ecumenical Church will depend on the individual Christian. There can be dependable progress only where there is a sufficient number of men and women with the necessary quality of faith and life and witness to carry the movement forward.

There has been much discussion of the distinction between a "sect" and a "church." Without regard to the finer technical points, I believe it is possible to arrive at a working definition. This is not a complete description of the difference, but it will serve to clarify a major distinction. An organized body of Christian believers which receives new members with the understanding that they are being brought into the fellowship of all the followers of Christ, the universal Church, is a Christian church. This is true whether it has a membership of five thousand or fifty million. An organized body of Christian believers which receives new members with the understanding that they are being received only into the fellowship of that particular branch of the Church is a Christian sect. This is true, again, whether it numbers its members by hundreds or millions. Sectarianism is not a matter of size but of spirit and outlook. If this distinction is valid, every pastor should ask himself this question at frequent intervals: "Is the congregation which is committed to my care being led to regard itself as a part of a Christian sect or a part of the Universal Christian Church?" And the question needs to be asked regardless of the denomination to which the congregation belongs. Men are sometimes larger, sometimes smaller, than the denominational structure in which they serve. Co-operation across denominational lines becomes easy and logical when individual Christans have been nurtured in the understanding that these divisions are largely matters of historic backgrounds and varying emphases and that they do not annul the essential unity of the household of Christ.

Intelligent co-operation

A second field of activity which is open to pastors today is in giving the fullest possible encouragement to all forms of interchurch co-operation in which church members can work together, across denominational lines, for social, educational, moral, and religious progress. The important fact to be kept in mind is that efforts at some type of church union or intelligent co-operation are not academic pursuits that have been initiated by churchmen who had nothing better to do. These efforts are a response to a condition, not a theory. They have been made imperative by situations in which the present mode of church life is intolerable. I mean to say it is intolerable unless the Protestant churches of America are willing to continue their approval of a pattern of community life which is divisive of basic loyalties, wasteful in its requirements of property maintenance and pastoral oversight, and a direct denial of the essential unity of the Christian Church. This is not an overstatement of the plight in which several thousand villages and small towns in America find themselves today. In a community in which the population and material resources are sufficient for the adequate support of only one church, there are two, three, and occasionally four churches—churches that are so substantially alike in doctrines and modes of expression that no sound justification for duplication can possibly be found.

The primary question in a situation like this is, "What is happening to the people?" One of the results is that the members of these competing congregations cannot escape the feeling of futility in much that is done in their churches. Membership and attendance will necessarily be small and the expense of building upkeep and pastoral support correspondingly large. The more thoughtful members of these struggling churches will be uncomfortably aware that the institution which more than all others should have united them has in reality divided them. The children of the churches are together in such community activities as the public school and character-building organizations but are separated when they come to worship and to study the teachings of Jesus. The pastors of these churches, one or more of whom usually live outside the parish, are even more aware of the divisiveness and the waste of energy in which they are compelled to participate.

Inadequate financial support presents a serious problem for a pastor with a growing family.

But the consciousness of poorly employed talents is even more disheartening. A seminary professor writes, "Pastors in these over-small, static, competitive parishes too often lose the vision of their great calling, become disheartened, and seek an escape from their difficulties by a move to another field. I think the financial is one of the least of the reasons for their restlessness. They want to feel more useful; they seek opportunities more challenging and stimulating." [2] Many a theological graduate has gone to a small parish with high hopes and youthful enthusiasm only to find himself confronted with a competitive church life that has brought disillusionment and a sense of frustration. This kind of unholy rivalry presents to the unchurched element of the community not a revelation but a distortion of what the Church is meant to be. Unity was a powerful element of strength in the early Church. It was a sign of its divine origin and a symbol of its unique ministry to mankind. It would be impossible to estimate fully the extent of the perplexity and bewilderment which have resulted from the confusion of tongues emanating from a divided Protestantism.

But there is another side to this unhappy situation of too many churches. It is found in the poorer sections of the cities and in the sparsely populated areas of the rural territory. It is estimated that country churches are being closed annually at the rate of from two to four per cent of the total number. Divided resources resulting from

[2] Walter S. Davidson, "The Plight of Rural Protestantism," *Religion in Life,* summer, 1946, p. 381.

competition causes denominations to withdraw in times of economic uncertainty and ministerial shortage. The outcome of this retreat is that in some sections of this country whole counties are left without a single congregation that is related to an established Protestant communion. With no dependable procedure for allocating responsibility in these neglected areas one of two things happens. Transient religious sects move in, or the people are left without religious instruction.

This can be done now

What can be done by intelligent churchmen—ministers and laymen—in the twelve or fifteen largest Protestant churches in America to remedy the situation which makes such conditions possible? In attempting to find the answer to this question it must be kept in mind that some things can be done only at the grass-roots level, and others must be done at the place where denominational policies are formed. The times call loudly for bolder and more aggressive efforts from the leaders of denominations that are of the same family or are closely related in doctrine and polity to bring their churches into organic union now. If Dr. William E. Barton's call "Let those unite who will unite" was premature a quarter century ago, it is certainly overdue today.

In the absence of organic union the next best procedure is the merging of two or more congregations into one church, on the basis of the relative numbers of local members and other factors, and the withdrawal of oversight by the other denominations that are related to the merger. This step can usually be best accomplished where there is an exchange of denominational leadership in two or more communities. Such exchanges, however, are not always possible and should not be held to as an invariable condition to this action. The loss of individual members can be kept to a minimum if sufficient preparation for the merger is made locally and if the proper kind of encouragement from overhead is given. Such losses as may occur must be measured in the light of the larger gains that will come with the next generation.

This is the place for a word about the obligations of the Church in sparsely populated sections from which Protestantism has retreated. Under the direction of the state council of churches this territory should be assigned to the communions that affiliate with the council on the basis of their relative strength and with the understanding that the denominations which accept this trust will provide suitable houses of worship and a trained ministry at designated points. Annual inquiry should be made by the proper committee of the council to determine whether this is being done. With a shortened missionary line resulting from this strategy and with more ready support from laymen who could then be interested in a non-competitive plan of church extension, the shame of these neglected areas could be removed. There is nothing new about this proposal. Such a plan has been in operation in the overseas work of the Church for more than fifty years and has resulted in vast savings in missionaries and equipment. Why can we not employ the same principle of co-operation in America?

Next in order of desirability to the merging of congregations is the federated church. Although there would be a minimum of dissent, I believe it is generally conceded that the federated church is to be regarded as a temporary expedient to relieve a situation in which a merger is not practicable at the time. It would be most unsatisfactory as a permanent arrangement to require each new member of such a church, particularly the children, to decide whether he would be, for example, a Congregationalist or a Presbyterian. The likelihood of friction and dissension can be greatly reduced by a plan of federation which is carefully drawn in the light of forty years of experience in this type of co-operation and is fully understood by the federating congregations.

The nondenominational church is not proposed here as a satisfactory solution of the problem of overchurched communities. The difficulties of securing a dependable ministry and of keeping alive the sense of world fellowship which is essential to true Christianity are almost insurmountable. This is true in spite of the fact that in a few instances pastors who have been trained in an ecumenical atmosphere and who have a world outlook have organized community congregations that are notable exceptions.

Don't ignore human nature

In the final reckoning each of these proposals is limited in its possibility of fulfillment by the mood and spirit of individual church members. And that mood and spirit are more largely than we like to believe the result of the convictions and attitudes of the men who are giving pastoral leadership to the people. The vast improvement in interchurch relations from the days of acrimonious debates and strict exclusiveness to these more harmonious

108

and fraternal relations is to be attributed largely to the changed outlook on the part of the ministry. The fact that there are still with us areas of unchristian exclusiveness means that the work of grace has not yet been fully accomplished. The attitude of the pastor in matters of interchurch relations will to a large degree become the attitude of any typical congregation in a period of ten years and in many instances in far less time. And the shaping of this point of view will not be the result of what the pastor says so much as of his total behavior where relations with other ministers and other congregations are involved.

Does he take an active part in the ministerial association of his city or community? Does he occasionally exchange pulpits across denominational lines? Does he encourage his people to enter heartily into interchurch community enterprises for which there will be no denominational credit? Is he interested in giving to his congregation encouraging accounts of the achievements of other denominations? Does he use the teaching facilities of the church and frequent reference in preaching to let his people know something of the common historical backgrounds of the churches and to acquaint them with outstanding leaders in other communions? These are some of the ways in which a pastor can declare his faith in the basic unity of the church in a more positive manner than by any amount of lip-service which is not matched by supporting action.

And if he were thinking in no wider terms than the development of his own people, how else could a pastor cause them to know that all things were theirs "whether

Paul or Apollos or Cephas" or Augustine or Francis or Luther or Calvin or Knox or Bunyan or Wesley—how would one know where to stop? What could be more profitable to a congregation of Christians at this stage of our Church life than to be informed of the range and sweep of the ecumenical movement? Through a series of sermons or forum addresses or classroom discussions it would be possible to acquaint them with the thrilling story of how the Spirit of God has been guiding his people in this century as he did in the first century when the first church council was called to meet in Jerusalem to determine the policies by which the infant Church was to be guided. When a pastor stands before his congregation to preach, he is there as a representative of a universal, supranational Church, which is no longer merely a dream and a hope but, in a very real sense, a living fact. Edinburgh, Stockholm, Lausanne, Jerusalem, Oxford and Edinburgh, Madras—the conferences which bear the names of these cities mark the long road of steady advance toward a Church that embraces all the races on all the continents. And out of it all there emerges the World Council of Churches and Amsterdam. What will come of that conference and of the plans and policies it brought to birth? Only the future can answer. But of this much we can be certain: More largely than with any other group in the world, the answer to this question is in the keeping of the pastors of the Protestant churches in America.

Redirecting denominational loyalty

One of the chief hindrances to church union or cooperation is the difficulty of redirecting denominational loyalty toward the more inclusive body of Christians. Every pastor who has attempted to lead his congregation into interchurch enterprises knows how meager is the response of many of his members to any movement which crosses the denominational line. And this fidelity is a positive force in the growth of the Kingdom which the Church cannot afford to sacrifice. It has been a factor in the unyielding courage which has made the Church an aggressive force at dangerous outposts from which it would otherwise have retreated. The problem which faces the pastor who takes this part of his commission seriously rather than following the line of least resistance is how to conserve this allegiance and direct it toward the larger fellowship. This will not in all instances be an easy task. But it is so essential to the maturity of the individual Christian that it can be undertaken with enthusiasm. It must also be remembered that in an atmosphere of full enlightenment the larger loyalty is easier to sustain than the lesser one.

Once, after I had given a talk on the subject of interchurch co-operation, a pastor said to me that he could not agree with that point of view. When I asked him why he objected his reply was, "I am afraid that if we associate too closely with other denominations we will lose some of the distinctive qualities that have made us a power for righteousness in the world." There is an element of truth in this preacher's reply that cannot lightly be put aside. And the statement which he made can be made by any pastor in any denomination. Indeed, it is being made— and with more positiveness in the smaller communions than in the larger ones because of their sense of a special commission. This is the barrier, more than all others, that is preventing us from getting closer together. The secret of its removal is the discovery that the qualities in each of the denominations that are distinctively Christian and uniquely powerful in the conflict against evil should be made available to all of us. An acquaintance with these qualities can be secured only by association across denominational lines. Our problem is to bring into the unity of the larger fellowship the best and most effective of all that has been wrought out in the history and experience of divergent groups of Christians.

Would it be too much to hope that there might be a group of preachers in each of the major denominations of the Protestant family of churches who would set themselves with unyielding resolution to the promotion of this Christ-inspired mission? It will require men who will refuse to become discouraged, men who will not accept defeat on one sector as the final verdict, men who will not grow weary in the toilsome process of claiming, if it be a foot at a time, enlarged areas of common ground upon which all of the followers of Christ can stand together. Such a pursuit would be a high calling, and the rewards in terms of inner satisfaction and the advancement of Christ's Kingdom would be greater than can readily be conceived.

Christ above all

Out of all the travail of soul in the search for ways of bringing together the sundered elements of the Church, this one overarching fact has emerged: The reuniting of the divided Body of Christ can never advance more rapidly than his followers are willing to give to him the place of pre-eminence. It is only when we stand in the presence of his transcendent greatness that the relative pettiness of our theological interpretations and of our variant methods of administration become apparent. Only then are we ready to surrender the smaller custom with which we have become familiar in the interest of the larger conformity. More than one man who participated in the conferences which resulted in the re-uniting of three bodies of Methodists reported that there were times when the proceedings seemed to be lifted out of the hands of the commissioners and carried forward by One whom they were seeking to serve. Something comparable to this must be realized, again and again, if progress is to be dependable and permanent. Without discounting the value of carefully formulated plans of co-operation or union, it must always be understood that the creative power of the spirit of Christ is as indispensable in the uniting of a divided Church as it was in its original generation. And the recognition of this fact must not be confined to the uniting conventions; it must somehow be brought to the local congregations if union is to be anything more than an arbitrary bringing together of discordant elements.

Before we are in position to rely fully upon divine aid, there are two questions we must answer, however much we may seek to avoid them or to phrase them in less decisive terms. The first is, "Am I seeking, primarily, to add new members to my denomination or to bring individuals and families into fellowship with Christ?" I know, of course, what the stock reply is but the answer of the heart is more important than the response of the lips. The second question is, "Am I willing for my denomination to lose its identity if such a confluence of ecclesiastical streams would be to the glory of God and for the blessing of the people?" Our first impulse is to evade the question by insisting that whatever is to the advantage of our particular denomination is by the same token favorable to the growth of the Kingdom. But the day will come in America, as it has already come in other countries, when this question will cease to be a theoretical one. Our answer should be prompt and without reservations.

The price of freedom

One further word needs to be said. What the future may hold for the uniting of Protestantism we cannot say, but it is a practical certainty that the pastors of this present generation will exercise their ministry within the pattern of the denominational plan of church life. If representatives from all the major Protestant bodies in America should assemble tomorrow under instructions to formulate a plan of union, it would require more years to agree upon such a plan and to put it into operation than most pastors now living have before them in active service. The larger divisions of the Methodist Church, with almost no differences in doctrine and church polity, maintained separate organizations for more than seventy-five years after the chief cause for separation had been removed, with the last twenty-five years of that period marked by serious negotiations in the direction of union. It is now quite evident that if the process had been consummated on the basis of earlier plans, minorities would have been left behind of such proportions as to constitute disunity instead of union. In view of the urgency for haste I do not wish to sound a pessimistic note as to how fast we can travel, but a realistic understanding now may save us from needless disillusionment and disappointment later on. The process of uniting the divided Protestant groups will not be speedily accomplished. Since this is the case it would be sheer folly for a man to waste his energy in constant irritation with a condition whose removal he cannot greatly hasten. Without lessening his efforts in the interest of closer relationships with other communions he will do well to accept the position that "we best serve the Great Church as we serve faithfully that branch of it in which we have been placed, but it is permitted to us, wherever we be, to chafe at the limitations imposed upon us by the divisions of the Church, and to love where we cannot at present share." [3]

It should be remembered that our denominational divisions are the price we pay for religious freedom. An excessive price it has been at times, and one which intelligence and a larger devotion could have greatly reduced. But even at its worst it has been preferable to bondage and stagnation. Totalitarianism in ecclesiastical organization as in government moves in the direction of coercion and tyranny. Dr. John A. Mackay, who has had wide opportunity to observe the operation of this principle in South America, reminds us that wherever the Christian way of life has been limited in its expression to a single

[3] Nathaniel Micklem, *What Is the Faith* (Abingdon-Cokesbury Press), p. 19.

organization, such a church tends to lose its vitality and to become a very unspiritual form of Christianity. It is a significant fact that the branch of the Church which has been most insistent upon having special privileges in matters educational and political in countries where its members are in the majority is today having its greatest difficulty in areas where it has long exercised almost complete religious control, and its largest prosperity in the nation where, by constitutional limitations, it is deprived of such preference.

Unity in diversity

The pastor must be on guard against an unwarranted defense of the denominational system in areas where better methods of working together can be found. But he must also understand that a considerable amount of the decrying of sectarian divisiveness by those who are outside the Church is an effort to excuse their failure to take hold of the task of making the community Christian at the only place which is now open to them—a denominational church. They persist in holding the image of bitter and destructive competition between the denominations which in all but a few isolated instances has ceased to exist. They sometimes assert their freedom of sectarianism by organizing undenominational community churches only to find that in the choice of a ritual, the administering of the sacraments and the maintenance of a semblance of world fellowship they are paralleling the procedures of the denominations without enjoying the benefits of their association. Dr. Elton Trueblood is aware of the sin of an exclusive sectarianism but he also knows that "we naturally form into groups and find our best life in reasonably small fellowships. Like-minded fellowships in different committees strengthen one another in conscious loyalty to a heritage. Such groups are called denominations. There is nothing very dangerous or surprising about this, and certainly there is nothing about it that is unique to religion. We do it in everything else, as the existence of lodges, political parties, and service clubs so abundantly testifies. It is very curious, indeed, that a man who takes for granted the existence of separate organizations for Rotary, Kiwanis, and Lions Clubs should profess to be shocked by the fact that Christians are organized in a similar way."[4]

Could we, after all, render a more effective service to the cause of church union than by making the denominations to which we belong more nearly Christian? There is a theory that the process of union will be hastened by the weakening of traditional loyalties and the depletion of denominational strength. I regard this idea as being wholly fallacious. Union and efforts toward union will come not out of weakness but out of strength, not out of sickness but out of health, not out of a defeatist idea that the Church is on the verge of a retreat but out of the conviction that the Church has a mission to fulfill of such magnitude that it can best be accomplished only by a body of Christians who are basically united in spirit and witness in spite of superficial divergencies. As we emphasize the essential and disregard the nonessential, the barriers that separate us will disappear and the bonds that

[4] *Foundations for Reconstruction* (Harper & Bros., 1946), p. 55.

unite us will become more apparent. We are like companies of mountain climbers who begin to climb from different points at the base of a mountain. As we ascend we draw closer to each other until, almost imperceptibly, we join ranks and go up together. And in the grand Hallelujah Chorus which will be sung at the end of the journey each singer will have the joy of recognizing certain familiar strains that have been brought up by the company of Christians who first taught him to sing, and with whom he has marched on the long pilgrimage.

VI

"I NEVER LOSE HEART"

How CAN A PREACHER MAINTAIN THE GLOW OF HIGH-heartedness and of enthusiasm for his work to the closing day of his ministry? There is no ready or easy answer to this, but I am certain that the most dependable source of light is the study of the lives of men who have found the secret. The pastor who fails to read at least one out-standing ministerial biography each year is robbing himself of that part of his heritage that can be of most value. Four such biographies annually would be better, and then he will not be able to cover the field in the course of his ministry. For a starting point, we go back across the centuries to the life of the great preacher of the early Church—Paul of Tarsus. There was a deathless vitality about this man's experience and his forceful re-vealing of the gospel that has sent men back in every century since he lived to light the torch of their faith from the flame which burned on the altar of his heart. The deep-flowing passion of his life made itself felt in everything he said and did. Across the years and over the barrier of translations his words still flash and burn. The recognition of his pre-eminence in Christian thought was never more positive than it is today.

The source of Paul's amazing spiritual energy is best explained by his own words: He was "alive in Christ." With full recognition of the distance that separates genius

119

from the ordinary levels of life, are we not compelled to say that this is the primary obligation of every minister of Christ in every generation? The central and absorbing business of the preacher is to be fully alive—to maintain a zest for living which does not depend upon favorable circumstances and easy success. In a word, he needs to master the secret which enabled Paul to say, "I never lose heart."

When life grows stale

"The Making and the Unmaking of the Preacher" was the title under which Dr. William Jewett Tucker gave the Yale Lectures on preaching. It suggests a field with which the minister will always be concerned. Any man who has had opportunity to observe the ministry from a somewhat comprehensive angle—or who has taken stock of the temptations that beset his own life—will testify that the greatest perils for the unmaking of the minister do not lie in the direction of the grosser forms of wickedness. The most common danger develops at the point where the stream of enthusiasm begins to run low and the preacher is tempted to settle down to the dull routine of mechanical performance. Gradually, and sometimes imperceptibly, his zest for living ebbs out as hopes fail of fulfillment and the petty annoyances of life find access to the inner areas of his being. The radiance of his first commitment is dimmed and the glory which shone around him during the early years of his ministry "fades into the light of common day." Upon occasion he may exert himself mightily, like a shorn Samson who has betrayed the secret of his strength and wonders why nothing happens, not knowing that the Spirit of the Lord has departed from him. He continues to meet the minimum requirements of the parish in an impersonal sort of way, but the splendor of his ministry has gone.

I do not mean to say that it is possible, or normal, for the preacher to spend all of his days on the mountain top of victory and exultation. This would be contrary to the deeper rhythms of life and would be out of harmony with the experience of those who have walked closest with God. Even the Master had his dark moments when he felt that God had forsaken him. There will always be a certain amount of unpleasantness and drudgery about the daily routine of the pastor. This is true with every man's work. But when he finds himself going day after day under a cloud of listlessness and lack of genuine interest in his work, the time has come for him to take himself in hand and discover the source of his trouble.

A temple of the Holy Spirit

One of the causes of a declining zest for living is a needlessly low level of physical vitality. The close relationship between the condition of the body and the moods of the soul has been so fully established that it needs only to be mentioned here. Without becoming a victim of a modern pagan trend to pamper the body, the preacher needs to remember that Browning was correct when he wrote, "Nor soul helps flesh more, now, than flesh helps soul!" However carefully a preacher may observe his devotional exercises, there are times when for the good of his soul he needs to see a doctor. The visit, however, should not be made, except in cases of acute infection or severe pain, for at least two weeks after the complaint develops; during this time most of the ailments will disappear. This suggestion does not preclude an annual physical examination which can be a means not only of revealing incipient irregularities that can be easily cared for but also of maintaining a health-mindedness which is an asset all through the year.

The truth of it is that any man who is past thirty must be his own best physician. Doctors can prescribe, but only the individual whose welfare is at stake can follow the directions. Nothing less than a definite will-to-health under the realization of its relation to an effective ministry can enable the preacher to avoid the pitfalls of overeating and underexercise and a foolish disregard for the requirements of relaxation alternating with toil. We are in a vulnerable position as ministers when we make a plea for temperance in one area of life while we carry about the unmistakable evidence that we are violating it in another area.

Wherever we touch the Hebrew-Christian tradition, we find a high regard for the worth and sacredness of the body. Many portions of the Old Testament relate to the laws of good health. Jesus gave much of his time to the healing of the sick. It should not be a matter of surprise that one of the secrets of the rapid growth of certain modern religious cults is the attention they give to faith healing and the maintenance of a high level of physical fitness. A careful weighing of the emphases in the Protestant Church would probably show that, in spite of the good work that is being done in its hospitals, sufficient attention is not being given in the local congregation to the close relationship between faith and health.

The real secret of achieving a glowing, active life is in knowing how to balance the energy budget so that the output is matched by the intake. The source of this exuberant vitality is one which each man must discover for himself.

It is not given to every man to have a robust body and a wide margin of physical energy. Some of the most glowing chapters of the ministerial record have been written by men who were compelled to battle all their lives with physical impairments and afflictions. Much has been said to emphasize the importance of good health as a qualification for an effective ministry. A word is in order concerning the distinctive ministry of those who through the mastery of their own physical defects have been able to give hope and courage to others. I am thinking, for example, of a young man who came home from Europe with disabling wounds and a face so badly frozen that it had to be remade by plastic surgery. But there is a song of gratitude in his heart and the feeling that God has something for him to do. In a theological seminary he is now preparing for whatever specialized Christian service may be open to him. I know, also, a special counselor for veterans' hospitals who was born without arms. Hundreds of maimed service men have taken heart from this man who scorns sympathy and asks only to be treated as a man. Instances could be multiplied of those who have achieved victories in a conflict which in greater or less degree comes sooner or later to every man. Sound health will always be a major asset in the ministry, but when the call of God is upon a man's life and courage is in his heart, even the handicaps of the body can be turned to extraordinary advantage.

The secret of vitality

The question of what is the best kind of vacation is a perennial one. A month's vacation may be a good plan or it may not be—depending on how it is used. I have never felt the necessity of taking so much time from my work. But it is never a good plan if the preacher attempts to make it a time for atoning for the neglect which he has practiced toward himself during the other eleven months of the year. The basic cycle of man's life is not twelve months nor one month—it is twenty-four hours. All that is required for body, mind, and soul of toil and rest, of recreation and worship, should be provided within that period. Since in most cases this cannot be done ideally, God has established another cycle, just above this one— the seven-day period. The religious principle of the Sabbath is grounded in human nature and will not be erased by an easygoing disregard for its sanctity. It is probable that the refusal to "remember the Sabbath Day and keep it holy" is the rock upon which the lives of individuals and nations have broken as often as any other. In Sholem Asch's novel *East River* the central character is a Jew, Moshe Wolf. In spite of all of his tribulations—and in the mixed and confused life of Forty-eight Street he had many of them—some things he holds on to. He comments on the Sabbath: "When a man labors not for a livelihood but to accumulate wealth, then he is a slave. Therefore it is that God granted us the Sabbath. For it is by the Sab-

bath that we know we are not work animals, born to eat
and to labor: we are men. It is the Sabbath which is man's
goal—not labor, but the rest which he earns from his labor.
It was because the Jews made the Sabbath holy to God that
they were redeemed from slavery in Egypt. It was by the
Sabbath that they proclaimed that they were not slaves
but free men. . . ." [1]

Since the preacher cannot observe Sunday as a day of
rest he must find another day—each man for himself. Some
men take Monday as the day. It is not as good as Saturday
for the reason that it is better to rest in preparation for
work than afterwards in recuperation from it. The proper
use of Saturday is the surest preventive of "blue" Monday.
It should be the preacher's own day. Interruptions will
come, inevitably, but apart from inescapable demands he
should do nothing on this day that he himself does not
want to do. It is remarkable how many vital ideas come to
a man when he is not directly looking for them. Strenuous
searching seems to frighten them away. But when the
tensions are off and he is relaxed, they come in quietly and
he needs only to corral them. Henry Ward Beecher had the
habit of riding the Brooklyn ferryboats on Saturday—
watching the river and the city and talking with the boat-
men and the passengers. He reported that this was one of
the ways he had of finding what Bishop Quayle would
have called "pollen for the mind." Nathaniel J. Burton,
in *In Pulpit and Parish*—which, incidentally, is still one of
the most stimulating in the series of Lyman Beecher Lectures on Preaching—has a sound word in defense

[1] G. P. Putnam's Sons, 1946, p. 408.

of the fine art of loafing: "Nature takes loafers into her arms and loves them, prefers them, and tells them things and soaks her own peace into them and smooths out their seemingly hopeless kinks and hushes their nerves and eliminates from their make-up their artificialities and twists of dishonesty that they get in society and sends them back home feeling like a wood-nymph."[2] If a day off can do that, then it is worth contending for. One sure formula for maintaining vitality—physical, mental, and spiritual—is this: Take a vacation every week. When a man comes to look back across the years of his ministry, it is likely that he will discover that some of the most rewarding experiences of his life came to him, not while he was seeking them but while he was, without intent, keeping open house for God's messengers.

"Lest I myself should be disqualified"

It may be that a critical self-examination will show that while the pastor was guarding the souls of others, his own soul was unguarded. It is a fact too well illustrated that constant association with sacred things is no security against the infiltration of corrosive evils. The men who most persistently opposed Jesus at every step of his ministry and who finally sent him to the Cross were the priests and officials of the church of that day. The best evidence that the disciples were beginning to understand themselves after being with Jesus was the fact that when he announced that one of them would betray him they each asked, "Lord, is it I?" Paul was not dealing in fiction when he confessed that he lived under a sense of dread that after telling others how to

[2] The Macmillan Co., 1925, p. 363.

chart the course of their lives he might make shipwreck of his own.

Leaving aside the temptations to the sins of the flesh, such as lust, gluttony, and laziness, what are some of the ministerial devils that plague the life of the preacher and rob him of the inner joy and peace which Christ wants him to have? There is nothing distinctively ministerial about the gnawing sense of fear which expresses itself in feelings of worry and insecurity. This is a common affliction. But in the minister it is more inexcusable because of his relation to One who taught that life was more than food and the body more than clothing. It is a decisive day in the development of any Christian, and certainly for the preacher, when, in the full knowledge of the hostile realities of life as well as its favorable ones he can say, from his heart, "I am not afraid." This is not a mood which a man can maintain of his own strength. It is not to be regarded as the subject of cheap exhortation from those who have no real cause for anxiety to those who live in the shadow of danger. In its most dependable form it comes from a deep confidence that no experience can come to a Christian that cannot be used for the growth of his own soul and for the glory of God. Peace of mind is not to be regarded as an end in itself but it is the atmosphere in which stalwart virtues can mature.

The demon of jealousy

Prominent among the perils that assail the ministry is the feeling of envy and jealousy toward a brother preacher who has met with greater success in his ministry and has moved into larger churches. The preacher who harbors this feeling compares himself with the other man and can find no reason why this recognition should not have come to him. It would be impossible to estimate the degree to which the effectiveness of the ministry has been reduced by this sin, but there is cause to believe that the loss is great. Most men who are tempted at this point are wise enough to look about them and to see that there are others who have not fared as well as they have. The demon of jealousy is thus mastered by the grace of gratitude. But there are some men who seem to look in only one direction. When the preacher lives for a time with a spirit of envy and disappointment in his heart, he begins to question the justice of the administrative system of his church, whether it be congregational or connectional. His loyalty to his denomination begins to decline, and a critical, censorious spirit emerges. In an atmosphere of suspicion concerning the integrity of his fellow men, the acid of doubt begins to attack his faith in God. The note of positive assurance begins to slip out of the gospel he preaches, and he wonders why. More often than we suspect, our doubts concerning God have their beginning in a debased conception of man. It was out of a true understanding of human nature that a New Testament writer asked, "He that loveth not his brother whom he hath seen, how can he love God whom he hath not seen?"

Here is one means of resisting this pernicious evil. More than twenty-five years ago a seminary professor remarked to his class that when he had difficulty in finding an idea for a sermon he always read again Emerson's "Compensation." Since that day I have read this essay many times and have found in it more than sermons. A satisfactory amount of freedom from the blight of envy grows out of the conviction that there is an evenhanded justice in the universe which sees to it that when a man puts his best effort into his work, what he loses at one point he gains at another. In the final accounting the books of God are never out of balance. I am convinced that the unreserved acceptance of this simple but profound truth would take the fever of anxiety and restlessness out of many a preacher's heart and would enable him to find contentment—not static but creative—in the place where he now is.

The poison of despair

Less vicious but scarcely less destructive is the mood of pessimism and hopelessness. The paralyzing power of despair can hardly be exaggerated. A completely hopeless man is a completely defeated man. Not even the omnipotence of God can use him until his outlook is changed. Whatever his gifts and talents may be, they are all like so many prisoners chained in a dungeon so long as his heart is in the grip of despondency. In the long trek which Bunyan's pilgrim made from the City of Destruction to the Celestial City there was only one time when he was completely disqualified for the journey and the conflicts it involved. That was the time when he fell into the clutches of Giant Despair and was made a prisoner in Doubting Castle.

The disturbing fact is that hopelessness is a spiritual virus which can be transmitted to others. The preacher cannot lock this attitude within his heart and keep it as his own secret—he is too much under observation. It writes itself into the features of his face, it finds expression in the tones of his voice, it reveals itself in everything he does. It would be hard to imagine a worse calamity that could befall a congregation than to have for a pastor a man who harbored a spirit of bitter disappointment or was inwardly defeated. The tragedy of it is that at the one place in the whole range of their lives where the people have the right to expect light they find darkness. Thoughtful men and women who sit in our pews do not look for superficial optimism from the man in the pulpit. Such an attitude in a day like this would reveal either ignorance or hypocrisy. But they do have at least a dim conviction that the Christian faith takes hold upon a wider reach of reality than the here and now. They feel that if the man who stands as God's representative has any word of hope and encouragement, he should speak it now.

Glib and assured antidotes to the poison of despair in the heart of the preacher are out of place. It can be said with certainty that the remedy lies in the direction of a renewed faith in the ultimate dependability of God. There will always be an element of daring adventure in the acceptance of the Christian faith. This does not mean that God is seeking to hide himself from us. It means that because of our immature and imperfect sense of spiritual perception he is not able to make so complete a revelation of himself that the element of chance is eliminated. It may be that the taking of this risk is one of the necessary disciplines in the development of a dependable faith. Two facts need to be kept before us. First, the Christian conception of the universe involves fewer problems for the mind than the materialistic view. Second, the most daring explorers in the realms of history, science, and philosophy are finding increasing evidence that this is the kind of a universe in which all of the facts can be accounted for only on the basis of the ultimate truth which Christ revealed. If we really believe in "God the Father Almighty," faith in the final triumph of his righteousness is the only logical consequence. "We, too, believe, and so we speak."

Keeping the sense of reality

Next in importance to a spirit of unconquerable enthusiasm for this ministry stands the necessity for a deep-flowing sense of reality. So many of the things which the preacher must do belong to the realm of the intangible that the danger of becoming hazy and nebulous is a constant one. The mystical revelation must meet the test of the practical requirement; the radiance of the mountain experience must be brought to the hopelessness of the valley. Emerson's preacher, whose vapidness was contrasted with the reality of the falling snow, was not the last man to stand in a pulpit and discourse about abstractions that did not remotely touch the lives of those who heard him. The Hebrew prophets and some of the early Christian preachers had the advantage at this point of using a language that consisted almost wholly of concrete rather than abstract terms. It is a significant fact that in the course of Christian history as many heresies have grown out of the denial of the essential humanity of Jesus as have developed from doubt concerning his divinity. It was an unerring instinct for the indispensable that caused the early Church to contend fiercely for its historical heritage. If that taproot should be cut, Christianity would wither and perish.

This, I suppose, is the reason why Jesus, himself a

carpenter, passed by the religious professionals of his day in selecting the men to whom he would commit his message and chose hardhanded fishermen, laborers, a tax collector and, if tradition can be trusted, a mule driver. He wanted men who had a sense of reality that was born of first hand contact with the simple, elemental facts of life. He seemed to have confidence that such men would never lose themselves in the fog of philosophical vagaries. They had what Paul calls "a sense for what is vital." With all of its limitless reaches into the unseen, the gospel as Jesus presented it always rested back upon the firm base of elemental things that the people who heard him were constantly dealing with—fishing nets, loaves of bread, vineyards, children at play, funerals, buried treasure, leaven, wedding parties, and all the familiar things that furnished the warp and woof of ordinary life. When theology gets separated from life, it is a sad day for both. For example, how can we account for the atrocious statements about God's dealings with nonelect babies that got into some of the historic confessions of faith? Only by understanding that they were the products of minds that were temporarily ignoring the reflection of God's nature in humanity at its best. They had forgotten, for a time, that God was a Father. The business of helping people to see the unseen is best accomplished by those who cannot forget that there is an indissoluble union between nature and grace.

There is a theory—probably a correct one—that during the thousands of years while man was dependent for his existence upon the products of his hands there was instilled into his nature a desire to make things. When this creative instinct is thwarted, as is the case with many people today, it becomes restless and causes various kinds of inner disturbances. This condition accounts for the release and satisfaction which some men find in working with their hands. I know a pastor who takes the sense of strain out of his soul by polishing into all kinds of artistic designs agates which he picks up in the mountains on his summer vacations. A woodwork shop in the basement or attic room of the parsonage can become a place where the by-products are more valuable than the things that are made. One pastor that I know makes baptismal bowls and gives to the parents the one from which their baby is baptized on Palm Sunday. Another has made an altar and other furnishings for the chancel of his church. Blessed is the man who has access to a plot of God's good earth in which he can dig and from which he sees things grow—things pleasant to the eye and good for food. There are those who affirm that such contact with the elemental, life-giving realities of nature which inhere in the soil can do more, at far less expense, to restore a man to a clear-eyed outlook on life than even the celebrated game known as golf. But I do not argue. Certain it is that many a pastor has developed an appreciation for physical toil—of which a vast amount is required to keep the world going—by feeling the pull on his muscles which comes with doing something useful and essential.

And there is almost no end to what might be said about intriguing hobbies and avocations in which men have found the opportunity to express a special gift and to turn it to an advantage in their pastoral contacts. I know a church that was so hopelessly in debt that the officials were offended by the very mention of their obligations until a pastor went to the parish who had a gift for photography and motion pictures. Largely by means of this talent he broke through the barrier of indifference and in a remarkably short time the debt was paid. I knew a preacher who found great delight in studying the stars. He had his own telescope and all the star maps, and he kept in touch with the findings of the great observatories. This knowledge of the heavens was a point of contact with the young people of his church. He remembered that Carlyle once said, "Why did not someone teach me the constellations when I was young?" Some of these boys went out later to fly great planes at night, and as they used the stars for range lights, they remembered that a pastor had helped them to understand that these were not just blazing suns but were parts of God's purposeful universe. Enough has been said here to emphasize the peril of unreality in the ministry and to suggest a few ways of escaping it. Each preacher must find his own point of contact, with gratitude that the possibilities are so numerous.

Freedom through discipline

Under the head of the minor afflictions that torment the preacher should be listed the demon of disorder. Few men are under call from so many different directions as the minister, and excuses for a deranged schedule are easy to find. It is possible for a pastor to become so completely the slave of whatever happens to turn up that he lives in an atmosphere of indecision and confusion. With no established plan to guide him he is without defense against the most trivial demands upon his time and energy. The one dependable barrier against all such encroachments is a plan of operation during certain specified hours of the day so solidly established that nothing less than a minor earthquake can disrupt it. Fortunate is the man whose date book is so well kept that he is able in good conscience to decline invitations that have no central importance, even though the person who makes the request might not always recognize the validity of the prior engagement. It is a notable day in a preacher's life when he discovers that the regularity of a fixed routine, which has often been regarded as a mark of bondage, can be so directed as to become the password into a secure freedom. Situations which require immediate attention will, of course, arise out of the unexpected. But the man who knows where the break was made in his fixed routine will also know where to take hold again when the interruption has passed. Dr. Paul Sherer, who can speak out of a more difficult situation than most preachers ever experience, says: "Mastery of our time may not always be possible. When everything is said and done, you and I are men under authority and cannot command our ways; yet to lose a battle need not be to lose a whole campaign. One morning ruthlessly torn out of your hands and away from its original purpose by some necessity that does not ask your leave may still be made up, hour for hour, if you really mean this ledger of yours to balance." [3]

The good fight

An insidious peril that shadows the pastor from the first day of his ministry to the last day is the temptation to become suave and genial to the point of losing all de-

---

[3] *For We Have This Treasure* (Harper & Bros., 1944), p. 149.

pendable effectiveness. The nature of his work makes this tendency inevitable. If he is really to minister to people he must live with them, must speak their language, must have their confidence. This means that he must cultivate the qualities in his life which make him agreeable and likable. It is natural that an appreciative congregation should say nice and pleasing things to him about himself and about his work. It is also natural that he should not want to give needless offense. His pastoral duties bring him into daily contact with the best people of the community. He must maintain a sympathetic understanding for old people and little children. A major part of all his associations pull him in the direction of things that are peaceful and consoling. And so with a little yielding here and a slight compromise there, almost before he knows it there is in the making a man who is harmless and, ultimately, spineless.

But there is another side to this picture. The pastor who is worthy of a place in this succession is, as the name implies, a shepherd. If he is a good shepherd, he knows not only the quiet places and still waters but he also knows the enemies within the fold and on the outside that can blight and destroy. If he has dependability and courage he will not flee, as the hireling does, when the wolf comes. However strongly inclined he may be toward the ways of peace, he knows that the element of conflict is in all of life. It is in all great literature. It runs the full course of the Old Testament. It expresses itself in the shadow of the Cross which fell athwart the ministry of Jesus and continued in the persecutions of the early Christians. It seems to be a part of God's plan for the growth of the soul. Without losing the sympathetic touch which enables him to bring comfort where it is needed, the pastor must develop a toughness of fiber that does not yield to the threats of arrogant and entrenched evil. The most disquieting of the beatitudes of Jesus for many present-day Christians is the one in which he said, "Blessed are they which have been persecuted for righteousness' sake." It will be to the advantage of the preacher's personal life and to his ministry if he begins early to follow Browning's admonition,

> Then, welcome each rebuff
> That turns earth's smoothness rough,
> Each sting that bids nor sit nor stand but go!
> Be our joys three-parts pain!
> Strive, and hold cheap the strain;
> Learn, nor account the pang; dare, never grudge the throe.

Less poetic but more direct is the counsel which an older preacher once gave to a beginner: "My boy, if you can find a good fight, you had better get into it."

But be sure it is a "good fight." Some pastors have involved themselves and their congregations in a vast amount of needless controversy because they have not been able to distinguish between a real principle and a marginal custom. They contend so valiantly and so continuously for matters that are of no great consequence that when a valid issue arises, their persuasiveness has been wasted on trivialities, and they have difficulty in making their people believe that this other really matters. He was a wise observer who said, "It is not courage but lack of sense that usually gets preachers into trouble."

It can be put down as an attested fact that when the preachers of one generation shirk their obligation to join battle with the forces of evil, the next generation must atone for their neglect or cowardice by spending a disproportionate amount of time and energy in conflict with vices which grew rampant while their predecessors were taking the way of least resistance. Nobody loves a reformer, as such—at least not while he is alive. And yet his work has been indispensable again and again in order that the moral order might assert itself with positive force. The burden would have been lighter if every man who has been called to watch over the souls of the people had been willing to face his share of the danger. This means that every pastor has an assignment to resist the powers of wickedness; if he refuses to accept this obligation, someone else must suffer for his failure.

There are issues today that are related to human welfare, personal and national decency, and international relations concerning which the Church cannot compromise without forfeiting its right to speak for God. However much this generation of preachers might prefer to walk in quiet places, they cannot yield to the temptation without bringing upon themselves the condemnation which God put upon unfaithful prophets in the time of Jeremiah, "But if they had stood in my council, then had they caused my people to hear my words, and had turned them from their evil way, and from the evil of their doings." (Jer. 23:22 A.S.V.) One of the guiding principles in the exercise of this function of the ministry is that the preacher shall make sure that he deals with facts rather than with rumors and hearsay. Nothing could be more disconcerting than for the preacher to discover that he had built—and released—his argument upon a false premise. Oracular pronouncements on controversial issues thrown off in the heat of public address can become quite embarrassing both to the speaker and to the cause.

It is well to remember that we belong to and are products of the generation to which we speak. Dr. Gerald Kennedy gives this word of counsel: "It is of first importance to associate ourselves with the people and let them know we speak to our own sins as well as theirs. Sometimes you will find a man who has so fallen into the habit of beating the sinners over the heads with hard words that he has forgotten how to comfort the sinner who repents." Superficial and cavalier handling of profound and far-reaching issues is not to the advantage of ultimate solutions. It is amazing to observe the ease and nonchalance with which groups of churchmen, mostly ministers, can adopt in a brief session a whole series of resolutions touching all the major problems of the universe. The preacher must never forget that he is not primarily a denouncer but an encourager, not an iconoclast but a builder, not the herald of a negative word but of a positive word. He is the spokesman for the Christ of whom it is written, "For all the promises of God find their Yes in Him."

My own observation leads to the belief that the most frequent source of criticism of the pastor in this area of his work is the disposition which some men develop

---

[4] *His Word Through Preaching* (Harper & Bros., 1947), p. 164.

to spend a disproportionate amount of time "harping on one string."

No man will go very far in the application of the gospel to the social order without running afoul the bugaboo of "politics." True prophets of God, in any generation, have never been frightened either by the warnings of those who were jealous for the "sanctity" of the ministry nor by the proscriptions of those whose domain was being invaded. They have kept the issues above the narrow, partisan realm and on the broad base of human welfare, and have refused to be turned aside from declaring the whole counsel of God. The pastor who publicly promotes the candidacy of an office-seeker is weakening his position and is inviting needless embarrassment. In such a political system as ours the identity of men and measures is never close enough to warrant this type of ministerial activity.

The final test of the preacher's right to speak the condemning word is the question which an older pastor asked a younger one upon being told of the fiery denunciation that was in readiness for the following Sunday, "But can you speak it in love?"

"But the people will not stand for a full and frank declaration of the Christian message. They will leave the Church." The easy answer to this statement would be that it was predicted in the New Testament that the time would come when the people would not endure sound teaching. It is more to the point, however, to say that even though it is a sad thing for a man to leave his church, it would be sadder for the Church to become so vacillating

140

in its message that if the man really wanted to find the road to God he would not know the way. The other side of this matter is that nothing can so quickly and so completely destroy the layman's confidence in his church and its ministry as for him to feel that his pastor is shaping his preaching to fit the selfish instincts of those who pay the bills. It has repeatedly been demonstrated that when a congregation believes in the basic honesty and sincerity of its pastor, the most valiant defenders of his right to declare the truth as he sees it will be among those who do not agree with all of his conclusions. Whether they follow his preaching to the limit of its implications or not, men have an inner sense of security when they can believe that there is among them a man who dares to speak his message as he receives it from God.

Finally . . .

"Even unto the end" was the measure of Christ's promise of comradeship to the Church. It is no less valid for the individual minister whom he has called. Perhaps God's crowning blessing to a preacher is a clear-eyed, triumphant faith when his face is toward the west—a faith that confirms the gospel which he proclaimed in the vigor of his early and middle life. Let me close this chapter—and this book— with some words from a man who embodies the ideal of a courageous, forward-looking faith which the years cannot dim. Dr. John R. Mott, in his eighty-second year and after more than fifty years of conspicuous leadership in international religious movements which took him again and again to every continent of the world, was awarded the

Nobel Peace Prize. In response to a letter of congratulation he wrote, as the closing word, "Let me reiterate what I have been saying in this admittedly critical time, that in the light of my world-wide outlook and personal contacts, I am convinced that our best days are before and not behind us."

This is the victory that overcomes the world: Our Faith.